Life goes on

Diary of a cancer journey

Sylvia Edwards

Website: sylviaedwardsauthor.co.uk

Copyright and Ordering

First Edition 2025
ISBN: 9798309412761

Swinton Writers in t'Critchley Hub
Manchester
United Kingdom

Email: switchswinton@gmail.com

Website: http://switchswinton.epizy.com

Ordering Information :

Published with Amazon KDP.
Available through Amazon and good book distributors or directly from Sylvia Edwards
sylviaedwardsauthor.co.uk

Acknowledgements

I wish to thank all of the people who have helped me along my journey in one way or another: my loving and supportive partner, Chris, my family and friends. I am especially grateful to the medical staff; surgeon, doctors and nurses, whose sincere dedication to their profession has enabled me to survive and enjoy a future.

Thanks also to Bill Cameron for publishing this book, as one of our SWit'CH writing group publications.

Thank you, everyone!

Cover design: Author

Table of Contents

Introduction

A strange topic to write about you may think. But then is not cancer one of the weirdest journeys ever undertaken by human beings? Research tells us that one in two are likely to get some form of cancer in our lifetime. When I first heard this statistic I was aghast - half of the population! Surely not: that can't be right.

Yet, while the word 'cancer' may place fear into the hearts of those of us who succumb to it, how lucky we are to be living in the modern world, with the NHS on our side. We hear many complaints about our NHS on the media. But where would we be without it? Imagine!

This personal account is meant to be positive, rather than negative. I feel lucky to have a happy ending - having reached my destination: almost as if I have travelled through a huge, raging storm and am now seeing a rainbow at the end.

My goal now is to keep on seeing that beautiful rainbow, as if it is implanted firmly in my mind: its vibrant colours lighting up my heart from the moment I awake to greet each new day.

Yes! I am here!

I am grateful!

And here is my story.

PART 1: The beginning - one day at a time

Life is funny. We never know what may lie around the next corner. All my life I have tried to eat well and exercise in the belief that looking after our bodies as far as possible is enough to protect us against disease: or at least lesson our chances of being struck down. I have never smoked. I have drunk one glass of wine with my weekend dinner. I have walked regularly, and until this strange journey began, have run through our local woods for half an hour most mornings, alternating this with my Joe Wicks workouts, especially during Covid. I used to do the 5K Park Run. I have done one hundred skips almost daily. A reasonable healthy lifestyle, especially for my age, I thought. How naive!

October 2022
I can't believe how my life has changed in the space of six weeks, from the results of a simple blood test that turned out not to be not at all simple. I had gone to see the doctor because of skin itching: something I thought may be due to a sudden allergy, my skin cream or washing powder. So imagine my dismay when the results indicate a significant liver abnormality. From a reading that should normally be below 40, my liver results read way up the scale at 491. Alarming! Yet, the same blood test show other results as good: iron and nutrient levels, from which I take comfort. My body is strong, I tell myself.

Yet, this seems surreal. I am a healthy, active 77 year old. How can this be? What does a liver abnormality reading actually mean?

November 2022
Around the middle of November the symptoms escalate. The itching worsens to such a degree that my continued angry scratching causes red weals, where nails draw blood. My urine takes on a strange orangey shade, as if it is dyed. My poo is paler and softer than usual. And why, I think, am I doing all this uncontrolled burping? I also fail to connect my much reduced eating with these other symptoms. For weeks now I have been unable to eat normal amounts, but had put this down to getting older. Around the middle of the month, I begin to feel a strange lump in my stomach. Indigestion? The Gaviscon does not help. Throughout November, these symptoms escalate and I am desperate to find out the cause.

December 2022

I receive a text from the doctor: my urine sample shows an infection. He prescribes a week's course of antibiotics. Fabulous! So that's all it is - an infection. I'll be fine in a week. No more of this dreadful itching. If only!

Further blood and urine tests. Suddenly things start to move. I attend the hospital for an ultrasound and CT scan during the first week of the month. The results are in a few days later and I am called into the hospital to receive the grim details. I am assigned a cancer nurse. Blocked bile duct? During his explanation, the doctor does not immediately say the 'C' word. I do. He uses the word 'serious', but I know what he means. Pancreatic cancer is suspected. I am in shock. How? How can this happen, I think? How has my healthy lifestyle let me down? I ask the doctor if this is anything I have done, or not done. He reassures me. It's just bad luck. At this point he tells me everything they know so far. The lump is leaning against blood vessels and can't easily be removed. It can only be shrunk by chemo treatment. The good thing is that scans suggest it has not spread - it sits in this one place. Meanwhile, I am given medication to help alleviate the symptoms - itching cream, sachets of nutrient-rich powders to take with water, and tablets.

15th December

I attend the hospital for an ERCP. The nurse squirts yellow liquid into my throat and I have to swallow it: not pleasant but all in a good cause. I count five people in the room, all there for my benefit. I lie on my tummy, with arms down my side - then am aware of nothing more. A stent is inserted down to help shift the lump away from my bile duct (I think), and a biopsy taken. I wake up later in the ward, still drowsy from the sedation.

That night, is the worst night's sleep I have ever had. A lady in the opposite bed is shouting, calling out all night long. Though the ward lights are off, my bed is nearest to the lit corridor. Footsteps echo, while at intervals a nurse takes my blood pressure. I give in to the wooziness. It's the first time I have spent a night in hospital for years. And in spite of all the media hype of how our NHS is on its knees, I feel well taken care of.

It's time to go. Before I leave, Nina, the cancer nurse gives me a pep talk on the power of positivity. I listen and say all the right things, then look directly into her eyes and tell her about my daughter's cancer journey of eight years: multiple operations, a stoma bag, reversal op, chemo, firstly linked to a machine, then as tablets. I also tell her that Tracey got her all

8

clear only a few days ago. I feel sorry for these nurses. I couldn't do her job for anything, having to always find the right words in situations such as these.

Positivity. I should know what it means. After all our family has been practising positivity since Tracey's initial diagnosis in 2014. I think now about its connotations. The power of mind over body. Not giving in to this 'thing' that has invaded me. Counting my blessings. The glass half full rather than half empty. Finding the strength to fight. Looking forward to a bright future. It is all of these things and more.

The following morning, Chris collects me and we walk to the car, taking care not to slip on the ice. How weird that this experience of mine coincides with the worst cold spell for many years in our country. Minus six! How weird also that our beloved NHS is about to suffer from strikes this month, as Christmas approaches.

I reach home, apply my itching cream, take my tablets and think how lucky I am to have held on to my health for as long as I have. What must it be like to live with a permanent health problem, pain or a disability?

20th December

My daughter's birthday. Our lovely family gathers to celebrate and I think how lucky we all are to have each other. I also ponder on the likelihood of a mother and daughter in the same family getting cancer. What is the mathematical probability? During Tracey's cancer journey, the pandemic was in full swing. Myself and her neighbours left shopping on her doorstep because she was in the vulnerable category. Yet, we all survived Covid. I think more about positivity and realise something important as we all sit around chatting. Positivity is about love - the love of family and friends. Love IS life. The fundamental element of humanity? Love helps us to keep going through the challenges.

I explain to my elder daughter why I am not wearing a bra. It is tight and makes the itching worse so she offers to get me a softer bra/vest thing. Bless her! It's perfect, much softer and comfier.

The day after, I receive a copy of the letter sent from the hospital to my doctor. I didn't realise that patients are now told everything. The situation is laid bare. What was, until now, medical terminology: strange words with scientific meanings mainly obscure to anyone not in the medical profession and as emotionally distant as stars - now applies to me on a personal level. The words are frightening as I read this letter, mainly because they mean little to me. Yet these words and phrases are now attached to my body as labels.

A touch of the 'why me?' Well, why not me? I suppose I am as vulnerable as anyone else. I start to think about my Will. Is it okay? If only I have more money to leave. I feel cheated out of building up my finances for my family.

I think about my work. My latest Educational book arrives by carrier. Eight copies of 'The SENCO Survival Guide': third edition (twentieth published book). It seems odd that the first edition was published in 2011, second in 2016, and now this one, that has taken up a whole year of my time, from 2021 to 2022. I feel cheated because for this latest version, I have included a brand new chapter: of school and college research, that has resulted in me working voluntarily in a secondary school on their whole-school project to raise student reading/literacy levels: something I have thoroughly enjoyed, and, as a literacy specialist, was also good at. If only this cancer could have struck a few months later, I think. At least until I have completed what I am doing with the school. Can I get back to it once the chemo begins? It's another of those questions without answers?

22nd Dec

I have coffee with my friends, Chris and Judith and let them know the outcome. I know they care. We have known each other in the same writing group for some years. Friends matter more than ever.

I phone my daughter and we exchange thoughts. How strange that we can now mirror each other's fears and concerns through the same experience that now connects us even further than blood. I told her that the tumour measures 2.2 cm by 1.9 cm, and she identified it with her own, medium, bigger than she thought. I hope it does not worry her, but we know each other so well. She understands my physical and mental symptoms the tiredness, the worry and strain of trying to hold on to that elusive state of being that we call positivity, and I now know how that felt for her. Conversely, she now recognises how it was for myself and her sister when she was diagnosed, because as an observer she feels the same. I never thought it possible that a mother and daughter duo would travel on that same cancer road. Who would?

23rd Dec

I attend the funeral of my ex-sister in law who has passed away at the age of 89. She would have reached 90 in February. We had planned a family party. I have known Marion for over fifty years, from when I first married in

10

1966, and used to babysit her four children. The church is Methodist: totally different from the last family funeral: high Catholic. It's strange. I find myself unable to sing any of the hymns or say the prayers. Even 'Our Father' eludes me. Why? The words are written clearly above us but somehow my mouth refuses to form them. Is it because I no longer believe in God, in spite of having been brought up a Catholic? Somehow the words appear blasphemous to me, as a non-believer. It is the same with Christmas carols being played incessantly on the radio. I cannot bear to listen to any more.

Later, at the Wake, our small branch of this much larger tree meet up with Marion's family members who we have not seen for years. It's catch up time: finding out who is who amongst the younger additions. As we leave, we joke about only ever meeting up with outer family at weddings and funerals. I wonder which will happen first? I hope my recently engaged elder daughter soon gets on with tying the knot - I don't relish the alternative.

25th Dec and 26th Dec
We spend this at the home of my daughter's fiancé: myself, my partner, and both daughters. My granddaughters are with their dad, as he and Tracey are separated, and they take it in turns to have the children for Christmas Day. Later others come round, the children are dropped off by their dad, and we all play 'Articulate'. For years we have been a family who play games, and long may it continue. It's great fun.

On Boxing Day, there are ten of us in our house, and this year, because I am unwell, we have planned to share out the meal. Myself and Chris do the turkey and stuffing. One daughter brings roast potatoes and pigs in blankets, another, mash. My eldest granddaughter brings cheeses and crackers, and we all pitch in. Surprisingly, it works well. Even my partner, Chris, admits it takes the stress away from us a little.

We take a long time to open presents, one by one: part of our Christmas routine. I become quite emotional as I open my lovely gifts and realise the love and thought that has gone into each one. I try not to cry. But sense our family love pervading the room like a scented candle. Perhaps it's just me, being over emotional because it may be my last Christmas. No! No! I will be here next year. I will!

My family! Small but precious. I cannot bear to leave them so soon. I am not ready. Seventy eight is too young. I want, need, to see my younger granddaughters grow up and achieve. And a great grandchild from my eldest (aged 27) would be lovely. I think about life and about health: particularly those Holocaust survivors who have lived extraordinarily long lives in spite of having been almost starved in concentration camps. What amazing strength and determination! Mind over body!

27th and 28th Dec
I sit up in bed, reading until lunchtime. I am in a lazy mood. Something tells me I should get up, go for a walk and start the day with exercise. But my book beckons. It's a real page-turner, a thriller. I can crawl inside and hide for a while, think about someone else's problems, though fictional.

My cancer nurse phones and confirms the diagnosis. It is definitely cancer. But I knew anyway, didn't I? Was there perhaps just a tiny, tiny chance that the biopsy sample would show otherwise? So now I am under the specialist cancer hospital for our area - Christie's. Either the 3rd or the 10th of January, Gemma, my nurse, informs me.

29th Dec
I receive a lovely email from my friend, Veronica, who has a way with words that is funny and caring at the same time. Her comforting words warm my heart as effectively as a hot water bottle clasped to my chest.

We go out to buy new bedding for our guests. My partner's brother and his wife are coming up from London for three nights. We don't see much of them, so I am looking forward to the visit, in spite of being afraid. I hope I don't embarrass myself.

Strange things are happening to me. My bowels are so loose, I must visit the toilet the moment I get out of bed - so I hope that our two loos are not occupied at once while our visitors are here. I have been wearing one of those incontinence knickers overnight as I had a near miss one morning. Fingers crossed. I have the strangest cough that seems to come from way below the throat. I burp constantly. When the itching starts I have to 'cream up'. It seems as though once one area begins to itch, another starts - ankles, calves, legs, thighs, and every other area, including the scalp - like a swarm of ants crawling over my skin. There is nothing at all glamorous about illness. I feel as if I have aged overnight. Dignity matters less than comfort.

The nurse (and my daughter) tells me to drink water all the time. So I do a tally in my notebook - the goal being ten glasses per day. Most days I manage six or seven.

I never imagined succumbing to daytime TV but can't read all day long. Yesterday I watched Bridget Jones's Baby. Today, I watched Dr Zhivago (Netflix). It made me think hard about the hardships caused by war or revolution, in this case the overthrowing of the Russian Czar, over a hundred years ago by the Bolsheviks. Now, via the news, we hear that Russian air strikes have left 90% of people in Lviv without power. I cannot imagine it - cold, snow, darkness - both actual and emotional. For what? How can any of us normal people understand the thrust for power that spearheads man's inhumanity to other humans? Is Putin an animal in disguise? I recall having a conversation with my fellow writers about whether someone should get rid of him. One person in our group believes that taking any life is wrong, even an evil one. But is it, if for the greater good, the removal of one saves millions?

30th Dec
It's 7.30 am. I lie, listening to the silence and wishing time would stop for a while. There is peace in my darkness. At this precise moment, the dark is more welcoming than the daylight that threatens to invade it. Night is, I realise, my escape from reality. But the clock will not stop. I know I must get up and face the day.

The Christie's nurse rings to confirm my appointment: 9.00 am on Tuesday, 3rd January, firstly for a blood test, then a chat with the doctor, presumably to discuss the chemo. It's the day after my birthday, when the family will gather to celebrate with me, as we always do. It is unfortunate that our sleeping guests will still be here on the morning of the 3rd, so will have to get breakfast and see themselves out.

Chris drives me over to Christie's because we do not know where it is. The 9.00 am appointment is so early I am fearful of being late and missing it. The traffic around Salford and Manchester is dreadful during morning rush hour.

Veronica rings for a chat. Bill, from our writing group has placed a picture of my latest book onto our group email. There it is! My friend Judith emails to congratulate me. She has also seen my other books on Amazon. And yes, I suppose seventeen or so educational books must represent something of an achievement.

Veronica is no stranger to illness and untimely death. She had bowel cancer in 2013 and has written her own diary of her journey - successfully beating it (Pain in the Bum, by Veronica Scotton). She has recently lost a son, and more recently, a nephew, who has lived longer than predicted, with Muscular Dystrophy. But more cruel, is the fact that her three year old granddaughter lives with Leukaemia, and spends regular time in hospital. It seems cruel to me for children to get this dreadful disease.

If *any* God is in charge, and if he is good, then why would he allow such suffering of the innocent? It defies logic. But then religion is nothing to do with logic, is it? One of the reasons why I have lost my belief is because evil is allowed to triumph over good. Evil people can live long lives, while good ones die? If God did indeed create us, was it an experiment to see what humanity would do and how we would turn out when left to our own devices?

On the way back from our visit to see where the hospital is, ready for Tuesday, it rained buckets. I could not help wondering if the rain represents God's tears. Is He trying to tell us something? Does He want to save us from ourselves? The sky was almost black. But in the wake of such heavy rain, the ensuing rainbow was one of the brightest I have ever seen.

31st Dec

My partner's brother and his wife are coming up from London. I am looking forward to it, in spite of the strange circumstances. I wonder if I can manage to stay up through the midnight hour and greet 2023 as it begins. We bring in the New Year with Jools Holland and I enjoy his rhythm and blues - my favourite style of music. I even manage a few gulps of champagne to toast the transition. As fireworks explode and light up the green outside our house, I wonder what this new year will bring. Will I see another? Yes, I will! Will the war in Ukraine reach an end? Will the world become a better place for the have-nots? I would like to think so.

My elder daughter is attending a New Year party. My granddaughter too is getting glamourised, as fifteen year olds do, to attend a party at her friend's house. My younger daughter has just taken the children for a visit to London. She is tired from all the walking around, so is resting: a quiet night in. The new year has begun - and so has my cancer journey.

1st January 2023

New day. New year. Can this be the start of my new approach to life? My positive approach to beating the enemy that has invaded my body? I need to prove that IT has not invaded my mind too. I watch the new film, Pinocchio: about love, and loss and change. Life is not meant to be pleasant and straightforward, is it? It's about responding to the challenges life throws indiscriminately at all of us - or to most of us, because almost everyone has a story to tell, involving love, loss and change. Challenges are meant to keep us strong - give us the energy to fight our demons, in whatever form they appear. Who was it who said 'what doesn't kill you, will make you stronger' or words to that effect? Do we all change as we move through each of life's stages? I can't help but wonder what the next chapter of my life will contain. My personal 2023. Who will write it?

2nd January

Here it is - my birthday. I am 78 today. We have always (laughingly) agreed what a silly day to have a birthday on, just after New Year. Didn't my parents even think of that? Sometimes I wish I had been born on a more convenient day - in May or October maybe. My partner's birthday is 13th December, kick starting the Xmas season, my daughter's is on 20th December, and mine seems to close down the festivities.

The family are coming round as usual, and this year, because we have visitors up here, my side of the family get the chance to catch up with Chris's, who they have not seen for some years. So another day of family love and lots of jollity. Another good thing of course - perhaps the girls will take down our tree decorations for us.

I have begun to exercise. Just a short walk around the green, but 'every little helps' as Tesco often tell us. A daily walk is now planned.

3rd January

A key day - I have a hospital appointment at Christie's to have my bloods taken. The start of my cancer journey. We set off at 7.45 to beat the morning rush. My first appointment is at 9.00 to have my bloods taken. The chemo cannot start until my bloods are okay and I am fit enough to take the treatment. Then we go to a different department for the consultation. I wait with my partner and gaze around the crowded waiting area. It hits me that every other patient in this waiting area has cancer of one kind or another - Christie's being a specialist cancer hospital. Cancer seems to hit people of every age. I know that I will be well taken care of. The thought is comforting.

My name is called and I go into the consultation room. My weight and height are measured, and to my surprise I am offered a cup of tea. The nurse enters and questions begin. What do I understand about this cancer? How do I feel? My lifestyle? Have I smoked? Do I have any family history of cancer? I tell her about my mother who died of lung cancer at the age of 76, and recall being so thankful on my last birthday, having passed that particular age milestone. I have always thought her cancer was because of constant smoking. But was it? Maybe it's genetic? Interesting. I mention to the nurse about my daughter's cancer from the age of 45. Somehow it seems relevant. I had never previously thought about the genetics.

The nurse checks out my chest as I am still coughing heavily. It's an infection for which I am prescribed antibiotics. I have had this violent cough all through Christmas and New Year. It's a relief to know what is causing it.

We talk about the 'bilirubin' count and how well the stent has done its job - my reading is down from 82 to 22 amazingly, and she is pleased. I tell her that the itching and other symptoms are much better. It needs to reach 20, but is at least going the right way. I learn that I have not been taking enough of my 'creon' tablets, which somehow help to direct the enzymes (nutrients) from my food to where my body needs them. The instructions on the pack say ONE tablet at each meal, plus snacks. Now she tells me that it's 3 with each meal, and 2 with snacks - treble the dosage. Yet, don't we always follow instructions explicitly.

The consultant enters and talks to me about the chemo treatment - a three month course, followed by a scan. If not shrunk enough, a second three month course, then further scan. If shrunk enough and moved away from the blood vessels it's close to, an op to remove IT. If this cannot be done, I am told it will be radiotherapy. It all seems so simple when I reduce the procedure into these few concise words. Yet, each word is laden with time and open-ended questions without answers. I now realise that 2023 will be mainly spent on battling this disease.

The consultant then says how lucky I am that the jaundice has virtually gone. He tells me it's a serious symptom and a major reason why my energy levels have plummeted. There is huge relief as I had not realised how dangerous and debilitating jaundice can be.

I have my date for the first chemo session - 19th January, presuming my body is fit enough. I think it will be intravenous, then maybe tablets? Bring it on. The earlier we begin this strange journey the better.

Talking about journeys, I realise I am unlikely to have my annual holiday with my family this year. For the last few years, myself, two daughters, and three granddaughters have enjoyed at least a week away in summer. In 2022 it was Kos. It has always been a delightful way to spend quality time with my beloved girls. Maybe this too, has reached its end. What will be, will be.

We get my prescription from the hospital pharmacy. In the corridor as we wait I have a horrific coughing session that feels so embarrassing, tears fall. It is embarrassing partly because of my weak bladder - having to cross my legs to reduce the leakage.

Home. There has been much to take in and absorb from today's hospital visit. I have already forgotten much of what the nurse and the consultant said to me. I feel tired, and lie on the sofa to rest. It's not that I have done very much except sit around in the hospital. But the emotional energy has left me drained. I have been given a package with information about what to expect from the chemo. I must read it.

4th January

I start as I mean to go on - a short walk around our green. Every little helps, so it's a first step towards getting fitter, however slowly. I think about going to a meeting with my writing group, but the coughing is so violent I don't want to risk spreading anything around. Besides, it's so embarrassing. So this is a day of lounging and reading my book. I'm hiding again inside someone else's problems. Nothing beckons.

I must tackle difficult emails. It's the first day of the new term and I have to inform my colleagues in the secondary school where I have been volunteering about my cancer. Perhaps I can still continue with my work there in some small way? I await their thoughts. Maybe it is not appropriate. We shall see.

It feels strange. Normal life has ceased, at least for a while. I am in a kind of suspended animation - floating around in a place where time is no longer a major consideration. I will be going somewhere new - and the chemo will partly influence when I arrive. So I will not fight it, but make friends with it - the weirdest health companion I have ever engaged with.

5th January

I awake with new vigour. For the last two days I have not 'been' and have been worried that something else is wrong as I am normally very regular. But this morning my poo is the most normal colour and consistency it has been for weeks so I give thanks. Is it because I am now taking three times the dose of those creon tablets? I also realise that I have not 'creamed up' for three days, am eating more, and my urine is more normal too. Hallelujah! Have I turned a corner? The antibiotics are already easing my cough.

For some reason I seem to have more energy and decide to walk down into the woods. I walk for nearly half an hour and return feeling refreshed and ready to tackle this significant life challenge.

Later I read the booklet the hospital gave me. Fear gradually creeps in as I read, threatening to overwhelm me with what *could* happen if things go wrong and my body reacts badly to the chemo. Anaemia, bruising or bleeding, lethargy, sore hands and feet as well as flu-like symptoms, affect

17

more than 1 in10 patients. Thankfully, less common side effects include - nausea or vomiting, hair thinning, diarrhoea, skin rash, fluid retention and sore mouth. Rarely, 1 in 100 patients may experience blood clots, chest pain or stroke, severe skin reaction and breathlessness.

Immediately, the initial pleasure I experienced this morning on *seeming* to feel better dissipates as I now realise the potential side effects of this treatment. Yet what is the greater evil - cancer or chemo as the means to fight it? Did I really need to know all this? It is frightening. Yet, by not knowing what to *possibly* expect, how can patients help themselves and know when to seek medical help? I realise that being prepared helps me to be on the alert, ready to take the right steps should any of these side effects show up. I also remind myself that these side effects are only *possible*. I may not get any of them. On the positive side, I may sail through this treatment with minimal discomfort. Or it may be a very rocky road.

I have also been given a leaflet on the 'creon' tablets and now understand much better the purpose of these and how they work. Why was I not given this booklet when I started the tablets? It would have made such a difference. I see what these enzymes are actually doing and realise their function. I also know I may be taking them for a long time.

It's strange because I now understand how my daughter must have felt as she went through her chemo - nausea, hair thinning, sore hands and feet and lethargy were all there, yet remarkably, she continued working. I recall her saying that the job helped keep her going, and now fully understand why. Maybe I too will need something positive, like my school support work, to distract me from what is to come. I will follow her lead and just get on with it, whatever this treatment brings.

I also read that my chemo operates as a four week cycle, a combination of intravenous, with tablets, for weeks 1 - 3, then rest for the 4th week. There will be six cycles. So I know now to expect 24 weeks. We will be into summer before this ends.

I suddenly burst into tears. I am a good and caring person. Why can't these things happen to the evil people in the world - for example, murderers and rapists? Then common sense prevails and I pull myself together. I CAN do this. I have my first appointment date: 19.1 for bloods, then 20.1 for the first dose of treatment. I am strong. I will be okay.

6th January

I receive my expected phone call at 9.00 from the MacMillan Nurse. The hospital has given me a booklet on MacMillan support. I wonder if I will need to use them. The nurse talks to me about my physical and mental health. I explain to her the irony of having to get fit for the chemo, only to have it render me (possibly) unfit again. She tells me that I appear calm and sensible about what is happening to me. I suppose I am. There is no point panicking. The more I can just accept this and be in control the better I will feel.

I enter my new year resolutions in my 2023 diary: long and medium term plans for the future. They remind me that I still have a future - and that it is entirely in my hands. There are things I want to do - continue my writing and publish more books, develop my media and marketing skills to promote myself as a writer, be in control of my website and continue with my school support to at least see the beginning of a whole school endeavour to improve the school's reading standards. Who knows: maybe I will be lucky enough to see such a strategy launched and fully up and running. I also want to sort out my personal life - perhaps to downsize and move into a small flat where I can spend my final years in a more relaxed and happy state, without the heavy maintenance of our ten roomed cottage, with its huge garden beyond our control. In short, I need to put my life in better order. Now is the time to do it.

I also have daily goals. For years, even when working, my goals have led me through bad and good days. The more ticks I put against my achievements, the better I feel. I now realise that this year of cancer will be no different. My daily goals will get me through.

On tonight's news we hear that Italian football manager, Vialli, has died of pancreatic cancer at the age of 58. My eyes fill with tears as I watch and listen to the report, and I feel numb. Here is a man, an ex-football player, who has been fit and strong all his life -now beaten by the same type of cancer as mine. The news item reminds me of the huge battle ahead. Fear sets in and I wish I had not heard this news.

7th January
I have spent much of the night reliving my many regrets: especially properties I could have purchased and let out to increase my finances. I tell myself this kind of looking backwards is of no help to me now and must cease. The past can never be changed, so why do many of us go back and revisit it? Such dwelling in the past is harmful: an emotional re-enactment of the daily flagellation used by medieval monks to seek forgiveness of their sins. What is there must be left behind. I am in the NOW and must find ways to move on into a future.

I so want to be happy, after years of being unhappy. This morning my partner wanted what he called a 'little hug', but I struggled to engage. We had a row yesterday about the house - again. We have lots of rows about this old broken down cottage that we share. He knows I hate it. But he loves it. That is the dilemma. I want to spend our days in a nice modern flat. During one of our rows he once said he will only leave this house in a coffin. So for eighteen years it has been stalemate. Now, I wonder where we go from here. One thing is now clear to me having got this cancer. I cannot continue to live in this cottage in its present state. The options? A flat for the two of us, or this cottage turned into a place where I too could be content and live out my days. What will it be?

8th January
Sunday. I lie awake during the early hours pondering on our future in this cottage. Could I be happy IF changes were made? This illness has highlighted the word CHANGE. I know without any doubt that this year will force my life to change in multiple ways. When I beat this cancer, and eventually send it packing, I cannot continue life in the same unhappy state I have been for years. I may be weaker than before, with less energy. I deserve better. My partner loves this house, but hates change. I hate this house, and need change. He has been happy here. I have been unhappy. It is surely time for us *both* to be as content as possible. I must be strong and stick to my intentions - the changes we need to make in this cottage are all part of the positivity plan that will create a future for us both, and help bring us back together in some way. So I write down my concerns in an email because I cannot get a response from spoken conversation: they end in rows. Change, especially in our home, is the one thing my partner resists - but it has to happen.

My daughters are popping over this afternoon for our Scrabble session, and my granddaughters will be dropped off by my younger daughter's ex-husband later. It has been his alternating weekend with them. We have a lovely Scrabble session, just the three of us. My younger daughter wins, she's our Scrabble champion, so the two us race each other. I'm second.

I have now decided to learn the piano. Some years ago I bought my granddaughter a folding key board for Christmas. I've arranged to borrow it. My goal, set by family: to play it when we have our Carols singalong next Christmas. Can I do it? Yes, I can!!!

9th January

I am determined to start the day with goals. So I go for my walk through the woods. Then I finish my email to C, about making changes to the cottage. I need to find the courage to send it to him, because I expect eruptions.

10th January

I am back in school to tie up loose ends from last term's project and discuss my involvement in their whole-school reading/literacy strategy. I feel excited about the possibility of continuing with something I so enjoy. It will help take my mind off health problems. We have agreed that training TAs to deliver reading, and Year 10/11 Reading buddies, may be a first step. So I can start to plan.

Christie's phoned to call me in for a PET scan, and Tracey tells me it will leave me radioactive for a few hours. I have to fast for six hours prior to it. I wonder what it will involve. I have finished my anti-depression tablets, and the cough has gone at last. I am ready for whatever this next treatment brings!

11th January

I remind myself that I am a writer - and that writers write. So I force myself to continue my novel - 12,700 words so far. Must keep going. I feel pleased, as if I have accomplished something. It's only first draft, but at least it's words on the page that can be fully edited and 'novelised' once the rough draft is completed.

It's Wednesday, my weekly writers' meeting is at 2.00 and I have not attended for the last month. It feels good to meet up again and discuss writing with like-minded friends. We are a diverse group of mainly older people, who write different things. Our new anthology has just been published, and I love the title 'All Kinds of Everything.' It occurs to me that this title also sums up myself and my own writing. I have been writing in earnest since 1988, when my first piece, an article on depression, was published by the (then) Christian Herald magazine. I have since lost count of the range and volume of writing I have done: twenty published books, plus short stories and poems, some unfinished. I wonder if some of these unfinished tales, written for adults and children, will die with me. But once a writer, always a writer, so writing occupies a significant part of my normal day.

12th January

PET scan day. I can't eat or drink anything for six hours prior to my scan at 1.00. So I nip down at 6.45 am for a glass of milk, with three slices of my favourite spiced raisin bread, finish it by 7.00, then return to bed. I think I can sip water until this afternoon.

I get up at 9.00, and try to do a few tasks to take my mind of the need for that lovely cup of tea I can't yet enjoy. I sort out washing, then clear out the spice cupboard to get rid of out-of-date stuff, and make room for new ones we got for Christmas. To my shame and horror, I find a jar with a 2006 date, and many more with dates prior to 2020. Sorting out old stuff feels good. It reminds me that one of my goals is to declutter the whole house - clothing, stuff we don't use or no longer works, ornaments I hate. I will get around to it bit by bit.

It's as if this illness of mine has heralded the need for a new chapter in my life. Yet a chapter without a clear shape - hazy and unformed. But will I be the writer of this new chapter? And how much of a horror story will it turn out to be?

We arrive at the hospital. I note the sign above the Dept 31 desk: 'Nuclear Medicine Reception', register and wait. The first nurse calls me in, takes my weight and height, and sits me down in a comfortable chair. Another asks me lots of questions about my medical history. 'Am I allergic to iodine?' 'No', I reply, hoping I am not. Then she attaches the cranula and I sit in the chair for one hour while the liquid goes in. I doze. Then, the scan itself. The nurse notices a bit of metal on my jogging pants, so I have to pull them down, and am given a blanket for my modesty. I am reminded not to move while the scan is on. This time it's a male voice that asks me to 'breathe in and hold it…then breathe normally.' I place my arms above my head. I lie, feeling quite comfortable, apart from a cold draught that seems to come from the arctic. Twenty minutes or so. I wonder how radio-active I am, although the whole thing has not been as bad as I expected. Two hours - done. My partner is in the waiting room, having enjoyed his lunch in the M/S cafe.

Home, and time for that nice cup of tea at last, with some porridge. I feel wiped out: not because I have done much. It's that emotional energy again that has drained me.

13th January

I decide to go for a walk but just as I am about to go out, it pours down again. So I abandon it, have my porridge and start writing.

I have an appointment today for my Bowen treatment, that I have been having monthly for at least a year. It's meant to relieve anxiety, by gentle and precise movements over muscle, ligaments and nerves, so generating signals via the body's autonomic nervous system, for the body to heal itself. I don't really know whether it's doing any long term good or not, but the experience is so relaxing and enjoyable, I have repeatedly gone back for more. This is my last session, as I don't know what the next few months will bring and don't want to make appointments I may have to cancel. Hannah, the therapist is so lovely, and she has given me a painting she has done. We will keep in touch.

It's amazing how things that people give us to show they care can help lift our spirits. The SENCO at the secondary school where I have been volunteering gave me a gift at Christmas - a little wooden, 'pocket hug' sculpted in the shape of a heart. It's beautiful and I will treasure it. It's good to know that people I have made an impression upon are there for me.

My partner and I go to see a film. 'Till' tells the true story of Emmett Till, a black boy aged fourteen, who in 1955 was severely tortured and murdered by two white men simply for speaking a little too freely with the man's white daughter, who ran a store in the USA town of Money. Emmett had meant no harm, and was just being friendly. From Chicago, where racial relationships had progressed to being a little more relaxed, he had failed to realise the strict separatist codes that still existed between whites and blacks down in Mississippi during that period, having gone there simply to visit his cousins. Emmett's mother, having lost her only son, subsequently spent the rest of her life campaigning for the rights of black people: thus leading to the 1957 Civil Rights Act, which gave some black people the vote.

The film was gripping, and watching it I felt a range of emotions, mainly anger because racial prejudice refuses to go away even now: about 170 years after the American Civil War. Our own UK history is similarly tainted. We have blood on our hands. I have written about this in one of my latest books, 'Time of the Virus', which expresses many of my views on modern civilisation. The stark truth is, in 2022, we are still far from being a truly civilised society. Watching that film, I felt ashamed to be white.

I look again at Hannah's painting and remind myself to get back to my own painting that I have not done for some time. Last Christmas (2021), I was given a personalised 'painting by numbers' gift by my younger daughter, fashioned from a photo of my three grandchildren. It is still not painted because I have no space in our dark cottage where I can paint. I need light. Also, as any true artist knows, such work cannot be tidied away after each session. It needs to be added to bit by bit. So, I need the one place where I could paint - our conservatory. But it's got a dining table in it that needs moving into another area. That is my next project - to reorganise furniture to allow my painting to happen. Exercising my creativity is even more important and will help sustain me through this critical period of cancer treatment, and I have many pieces from my weekly art club, unfinished, that I now need to complete.

14th January
Saturday. I realise with dismay that I am running out of my Creon tablets, and should have ordered them yesterday. Our surgery is closed, so I phone NHS 111. In a few minutes, my tablets are ordered, to be collected from a local pharmacy. And once again, I marvel at our beloved NHS. I know that our NHS will come through for me. I also know that in many third world countries, without a proper health system, being diagnosed with cancer would mean a death sentence. So I am lucky.

15th January
Sunday: I go shopping with my two daughters and two youngest granddaughters for a birthday gift for my eldest granddaughter. Lovely time spent with my family. How I treasure every minute. We have lunch at 'The Real Greek' restaurant and it reminds us all of our delightful last holiday (August 2022) in Kos. We discuss holidays this year, and I remind them that my family holidays, if abroad, may have reached an end as insurance, following chemo treatment, is likely to be sky-high. I have never been out of the UK without insurance. They suggest a long weekend with me in UK. Lovely. We will see how things are nearer the time.

16th January
Dentist: 9.45, just for a check up. I get up early to allow more time as the weather bulletin last night warned of snow and ice over hills, which stresses me out, as my practice is an hour away in Darwen, my birth place, at the same practice I had as a child. 70 years of the same dental practice! It is snowing over the Grane Road, which is across miles of empty moorland, but to my relief, I arrive well on time. My teeth are fine.

On the way home I do something so stupid I worry about it for most of the day. I misread a traffic light, thinking I can turn right, and end up driving the wrong way. Thankfully there is no traffic coming towards me. Yet if there had been I would not have got confused because I would have seen it, and known there was no right turn. This is not the first time I have got confused. I am a safe driver and well aware of other road users, but for how long can I continue to drive safely? I wonder also if I am insured to drive once my chemo begins. Must check this out.

I have lunch with my friend, Jean, a retired nurse, at her house. It is so lovely to talk to her. We are fellow writers and only a month apart in age. It's amazing how our conversation moves smoothly from one topic to another. I am reassured that she too feels more stress these days when driving. Very little of our conversation is on writing, but it's good to talk.

Chris comes back from his 'walking football' and mentions that one of his team mates will pray for me to get better. I think about prayer. Is prayer, regardless of whether God is there or not, more about talking to ourselves, empowering minds with inner strength and determination? If it is, then prayer surely equates to positivity: we are our own listeners. So I wonder, when I beat this challenge, which power or influence will have been the strongest - God working a miracle on me, inner positivity (self-directed prayer) - or highly advanced medical science? Mmmm? All three?

17th January
I go for a walk, determined to move myself off the sofa. It's bright, but the harsh frost bites at the tips of my fingers, even through my gloves. Then I write for the rest of the morning. It's amazing how good I feel when I have written something, regardless of whether others will read my words or not. Will anyone ever read this diary of a cancer journey? I hope so.

Chris and I go to look at curtains and tracks: a first start to updating and improving our cottage. There will be no holidays abroad this year, so we might as well refresh our house with the money we would have spent otherwise. It's a first step, and there is much to be done. We actually agree on the curtain material - but then I spy a rug. The colours match the new paintwork in our lounge perfectly. His face drops. I know what he is thinking. We bought our old lounge rug eighteen years ago, and he would happily die with it. Some psychology is needed. I decide that the best way to bring about my changes are to plant small seeds of thought into his mind, back off, and let them take root. The rug idea is now planted - I will return to it later.

18th January
Wednesday: it's writing day: actual writing this morning, then talking about

writing, critiquing and supporting members' writing at our meeting this afternoon. We talk about different writing styles: letters, prose, dialogue, as techniques for story telling. I read a bit from a novel that is entirely letter-based (epistolary), to illustrate the point. We then discuss the initial getting down of the story first, as sequential events from beginning to end, prior to 'novelising' the entire work through subsequent drafts. It reminds me that fictional writing is hard work. Will I manage to complete my own this year?

I am worried about my fitness, and don't want this illness to turn me into an old woman. Yesterday when I got back from our outing I slept for two hours on the sofa. I felt as if I'd run a marathon, rather than simply strolled around shops for a couple of hours. So it's time to get back to Joe Wicks. I start slowly - a few squats, planks and a bit of running on the spot. Let's do it!

<u>19th January</u>
It's bloods day. We are half an hour early for my appointment, and I wish I'd taken my book to read while we wait. My bloods are fine - so treatment can begin tomorrow. Then comes the bombshell: the nurse tells me the PET scan has shown a second cancer, in the bowel this time. I stare at her, trying to take in what she has just said. Suddenly, the shock is too much and I burst into tears. Fear overtakes me. Can my body cope with being attacked - not once, but twice? One cancer is surely enough for body and mind to cope with. The nurse goes on to tell me that this is a rare and potentially serious occurrence. I think about this. I have no symptoms of anything wrong with my bowels, and am absolutely amazed. I compose myself and try to remain calm. The bowel cancer can only be tiny or else I would surely have experienced symptoms down there. I now await a colonoscopy.

There is some good news, if we can call it that: the same chemo for the pancreatic will also work for the bowel cancer. The nurse goes through all the possible side effects from the chemo treatment. I brace myself for what is to come, and sign the consent form.

On the way home my fear is replaced by anger. Isn't one type of cancer enough for anybody! It's not as though I have been careless with my health. I've eaten healthily, kept physically fit, never smoked or drank - and done no other person any harm. Why has this happened to me? After the anger comes resolve. I can and will beat this. I CAN. I WILL. I MUST - for the sake of tho
se who love me!

20th January

It's my first treatment day. It's icy and slippy, but bracing. I walk, then write a bit, before we set off about 11.00. As we enter by the door where 'The Christie' is lit up in huge white letters, I read the word 'Christ' in the sign. Fear grips me again, but I pull myself together. I CAN and WILL do this - for the sake of those who love me. My mantra!

To my surprise the treatment is fine as I sit in a comfy chair, watching the news, while eating a tuna sandwich with my cup of tea. I can cope with this, I think. After the treatment, I am provided with multiple packs of stuff - my creon tablets for the digestion, as well as stuff for anticipated side-effects: anti-sickness tablets, mouthwash for ulcers and tablets to control bowel problems. I am reminded to take my temperature each morning and to call the emergency hotline if anything is not normal. I start to feel on high alert - as if a bomb may be about to go off inside me.

We walk out of the hospital with a huge pack. I am not used to all this medication: being ill is a novel experience. Yet, it's comforting that the NHS is here in my moment of need. I feel fine from the intravenous part of the treatment.

Once home I sort out the packs, and write a 'daily plan' for what I have to take, and when. We have our evening meal and relax, watching telly. I feel tired. My first chemo tablets (three, twice a day) are due around 10.00pm. I find myself staring at the pack ....then burst into loud sobs. I feel so afraid. I know what effect these pink tablets are likely to have. Yet, I also know the alternative. So I have my snack, take three tablets, and wash my hands immediately as the nurse has instructed me to do. Nothing happens of course, and I realise how silly I am being. It will take time for the effects to build up, and whatever they are, I will cope.

21st January

Saturday. I wake up and remind myself that each day is precious, and I must treat it as such. I feel okay from the chemo tablets. Nothing awful has happened, so I relax and take my morning dose, reminding myself of the 'good' they are actually doing. I have to book my blood test, to be taken before my next intravenous appointment on 30th, this time at St Anne's hospice, as it is more local. But there is no reply to my phone call. I may have to do this on-line - I hate on-line!

We go out and do normal things - post my granddaughter's birthday card, have lunch out and reorganise the date for the curtain man to visit as my changed appointment now clashes. I begin to realise that normal life will revolve around hospital appointments, and clashes are inevitable.

We do a food shop on the way home. It's strange, but my taste buds have changed over the last two months: I prefer softer foods. The lad at the Coop till gives me an odd look as he deals with all the individual rice puddings I have emptied from the shelf.

I try out my new thermometer, but don't know how to do it. The instructions seem so complex. My reading is 34.4? Is that okay, as it's below the 37.5 average? I have no idea, but mustn't panic, as I feel okay. I resolve to ask my daughter tomorrow. She's used thermometers lots of times on the children.

22nd January

Sunday. My elder daughter, Debbie, face-times me from London: she's visiting Paige, my eldest granddaughter, as it's her 27th birthday on Wednesday. I am caught out - sitting up in bed reading, unwashed, my hair sticking up, uncombed and without makeup. But it doesn't matter.

Then Tracey visits for a game of scrabble. Of course, she always wins, but how relaxing to play our game and just chat, even about the side effects of the chemo that she has experienced. Her tablets were apparently the same as mine. I am amazed as she tells me that ginger helps to relieve nausea. I love ginger biscuits, and resolve to get plenty in. She also books my bloods test online (I couldn't get through by phone, and I'm not an online person), and we practise with the thermometer, which today reads a bit higher - 36.6. What a relief!

Tracey brings the gift she has bought on my behalf for my second grand-daughter's birthday - she will be 16. I have lost all confidence in buying surprises for my family, as my choices, now that they have left young childhood behind, are certainly not theirs, so I just pay Tracey the money and be grateful I don't have to trail around the shops any more.

I think about the enormous differences between my granddaughters' world and my own at 16. No online! No mobile phones! No tablets or computers like we have now. How simple was my life when compared with that of teenagers today.

23rd January

Dr. Green phones from the surgery. It's just to see how I am and offer moral support. I tell her about the second cancer in the bowel. She asks about my side effects from the chemo tablets, but so far (fingers crossed!) I don't have any. She will call again in about a month.

24th January

I wake up feeling a range of negative emotions - anger, sadness, frustration, fear: that it's just 'not fair'. I try to turn these emotions into positive ones. The chemo WILL get rid of both cancers. I WILL live to see my grandchildren grow up. I WILL! My mantras help me to feel a little better, although I wonder if I am experiencing some of the side-effects listed, from the chemo tablets. My mouth is sensitive, though I can't feel any ulcers, but teeth brushing is a little painful on the gums. I am also burping a lot, and worry that the stent is starting to fail. Lethargy is also one of the listed side-effects and my tiredness is now constant. Most evenings I just lie on the sofa and doze.

However, I am driving over to my daughter's today, and picking my granddaughter up from school. Before I go I have to pay my annual subs for the art club, which I fully intend to return to. Art will do me good, and I have missed attending my weekly sessions. I intend to immerse myself in art far more, as I know how beneficial it will be.

This lethargy will not do! As in every aspect of life, this illness is a question of mind over matter.

25th January

I wake up with the intention of 'mind over matter'. The first thing I do is make a list of what I want to move forward with - my writing goals, marketing my new book and improving the house. My lists help to keep me going: otherwise I think I would just laze around all day, unable to get my head into gear. I realise that my head must be the driver through this temporary period of dense fog - not my body.

Wednesday: our writing meeting. I read the pieces sent online by members, and try to continue my own writing also. I have a novel that merely needs final proofreading, and email a friend who has the same. Can we help each other, I ask her? Can collaboration help us both to achieve our goals? Brilliant! Judith has agreed to work together to get our novels 'between covers'. It's given me a goal to strive towards. Writing has always been my strength, tugging me through life's personal dramas. So, by the time this chemo period is done (May?) - both our novels may well be published. It's a comforting thought.

26th January

A beautiful morning: the sun, directly in my path, shines brightly upon me, as I walk through the woods. It appears as a message - of hope and strength - the brightest light! I arrive home inspired, ready for a productive day. I begin to write - my novel, my diary.

I receive a call from Salford Royal, to arrange my colonoscopy appointment: 10.20, 9th Feb. The lady tells me that I can't eat or drink for 24 hours prior to this procedure. What? A whole day without anything - except water? Then she asks me whether I want to be sedated or have gas and air? Fear and dread creep in. My daughter has had a colonoscopy and I long to ask her about it, but can't because she doesn't know about this second (bowel) cancer. I dare not tell her: she has enough to worry about with her own health, as well as mine. I try to accept this and get on with my writing. It will be okay!

My partner and I go to Costa for a light lunch and do some shopping. A reasonably productive day.

27th January
Bloods day. I lie in bed getting more and more irritated at someone's car alarm blaring away, interrupting my last half hour of sleep. The noise lasts for at least twenty minutes as I try to relax, then is replaced by the sound of electrical cutting equipment: the gardener next door. I get up and dressed, and rant on about all this intolerable noise to my partner, who listens patiently.

I wonder why my skin is so red, and intend to ask the cancer nurse when she takes my bloods later. As I go for my short daily walk around our green, it occurs to me that this cancer, with its worries and escalating side-effects, is taking its toll on my emotions. I get irritable far more easily, as anger rises to the surface. I have less patience than usual. I resolve to be more aware of this and try to remain calm when things upset me. Positivity! My partner has suggested I try Tai Chi.

The bloods session is okay, but I don't mention my blotchy skin. I don't seem able to, as the situation at this venue is so different from the buzzing hospital. There is only one young nurse, and she seems distant, as if she just wants to take the bloods and go off duty - I am her final patient. I must ask on Monday when I go in for the intravenous treatment.

28th January
I receive a letter stating the date of my colonoscopy. Fear grips me as the realisation of yet more possible risks to my health sink in. With this letter are sachets of stuff to be taken. I will have to sign a consent form.

Perforations? Bleeding? This is one procedure I am not looking forward to. I can't read the information properly- not yet. My head can't take it.

We go out for the afternoon, just to get out of the house.

My friend Veronica rings and I ask her about the colonoscopy as she has had bowel cancer some years ago, and recovered from it - which is reassuring. Would she choose gas and air, or sedation? She suggests the former, referring the procedure to childbirth. But I'm not so sure I want the pains of childbirth at my advanced age, and with no child as my prize at the end. I dismiss the question from my mind. I'll decide when I absolutely have to.

29th January

Sunday: I awake feeling positive and determined to make this day as productive as possible. During the morning writing helps to take my mind off the 'C' word, and my lovely family are due this afternoon. I need their fun and laughter to keep me going.

I remind myself that when they arrive, Tracey can help me to book my next bloods session. It's a nuisance having to do this every week. I know I need to read my letter about the colonoscopy - but am dreading it.

A good family day!

30th January

I am due for my weekly intravenous chemo session at St Anne's clinic. I am determined to make this day a good one, in spite of what is happening. I must mention my skin rash to the nurse. And I must read my colonoscopy letter!

The nurse reassures me, my rash is just a side effect of the tablets. She also explains about the colonoscopy procedure - I have to take sachets and tablets to empty my bowel before the event. So, no going out the day before - I need to stay by the toilet!

I return to the tutoring I was doing before Christmas, with Nat, who has just turned 17 and attends college. Working with him on his GCSE maths paper does me good, keeps me focused, reminding me to keep going with normal activities.

31st January

A bright morning, and I start as I mean to go on. First my walk, though even that is an effort. Why are my leg joints so stiff? I complete a round of our green - about 15 minutes. Later I must do my squats, and stair runs! I am not going out today, so there is no excuse for not doing some small exercises. I can't believe it's almost February - about three months since my symptoms first began to appear.

I'm keeping going with my novel editing. It's great that Judith and I are pushing each other along - began Chapter 7 this morning (out of 47). Judith rings and we have a lovely chat about our writing. Should every novel have chapters? No, we agree. It depends on each author's individual style.

1st February

I make myself get up, at 8.30 exactly - my normal time. I lie, watching the clock, as seconds turn to minutes, realising how important time is. Once I give in to my lethargy and stop being taken forward by time - I might as well stop altogether. I am tempted to hide inside my darkness and not get up at all, having had a bad night: the itching has returned, interrupting my sleep. So it's back to the anti-itching cream. I remind myself that these chemo tablets, with their awful side effects, are in fact friends - annoying and irritating as they are - they are helping me fight a deadly enemy.

It's my writers' meeting this afternoon, so the morning is spent writing my own work, and reading that of others for critique. We have a good interactive afternoon. At the end of the meeting, one of our members, a devout Catholic, apologises to me for not asking first, but he has placed my name on the prayers list for his church. I reassure him, it's okay, and let him know how genuinely and deeply touched I feel. Regardless of our differing views on God and religion, I need all the strength I can get from strong believers. So please, bring on those fervent prayers! Maybe I too need to pray.

2nd February

I have the whole day to fill. Nowhere to be - so it's up to me what I do with it. Write of course, read, watch TV. The decorator is coming to size up a possible job.

I don't know what to do about a request from a parent to tutor her son. I don't know if I am up to it, yet don't want to let him down. I think he needs coaching through his maths GCSE. It's a bad day - one of those when I doze mostly, with hardly enough energy to eat. I am so fed up with myself, and reluctantly ring the parent back to decline the tutoring offer.

I phone Tracey and as we chat I realise how comforting it is being able to talk with her about stuff we both understand. I also feel guilty. She should be moving on from her cancer experience, not being reminded of it through mine.

I am so lucky. My two daughters are all I could ever want. When they were growing up, me having divorced their dad when they were little, we laughingly called ourselves the 'three Musketeers'. We were, still are, and will always be - *all for one and one for all.* That thought helps keep me going.

3rd February
Bloods day again. I awake full of fresh determination. It's raining so I don't go out for my morning walk - but devise an exercise plan. Today, *I WILL get up hourly* from my writing and do two minutes of movement!

I consider where my writing is going. By the time this chemo is finished and the cancer is dealt with, I may well have three books ready for publication: my historical novel, memoir and this cancer diary. How wonderfully productive is that!

My partner returns home with a lovely surprise. Bill, my Catholic friend (who is praying for me) has presented me with a bottle of Holy Water from Lourdes. My eyes fill with tears as I finger the tiny bottle, with a statue of Our Lady of Lourdes sculpted into the plastic. It is a symbol of hope and I treasure it. I will place it on my bedside table.

4th February
Saturday. I lie in bed reminding myself that I am breathing. I breathe more deeply, and rhythmically, as if to register that simple fact. I am here - and will be here for some years yet. I sit up, gaze at my bottle of Holy Water - and smile. Which is stronger - religious belief or medical science?

My partner, a dedicated Manchester United fan, is going to Old Trafford, so I have the day to myself. No excuse for not getting plenty of writing done! I walk around our green twice and feel good about that. Not much happens - just writing, reading, walking. But it's enough.

Before bed, I find myself holding the bottle of Holy Water and praying - but to whom - or what? To myself maybe? Does the act of prayer travel, not upwards towards the heavens - but inwards? Does God's potentially healing spirit lie deep within our own hearts, minds and souls? And is this where we draw our strength and courage from?

5th February
Sunday. My girls come over as usual. We play scrabble for a relaxing two hours or so, chat, then enjoy a meal together. Later their dad drops my granddaughters off at our house. I smile and listen, revelling in the childish

chatter and bubbly silliness of an almost-sixteen year old, and ten year old. How different is the world of children today. The older one is a little upset that her dad, who she sees fortnightly, has not bothered much about her birthday - having merely given her a card with £20. Men, eh? We reassure her that he still loves her dearly.

6th February

I try to be positive. Nestling my tiny Holy Water bottle between the palms of my hands, I sit on my bed and say a prayer. I have no idea who I am praying to, and my words are not from the Bible or from communal church prayers. But it doesn't matter. Perhaps my words are part of a pact I am making with myself to strengthen my faith.

It's my third intravenous today at 1.00. So I walk, then get on with my writing as usual. After the drip session we have lunch at Costa. Feeling tired in the afternoon, I doze, feeling shivery, and wonder why, when the room itself is not cold.

Later, watching the 7.00pm news, I find myself sobbing. Heartbreaking pictures of people emerging from rubble, some, including children, still buried, following the most severe earthquake for about ninety years in parts of Turkey and the Syrian border - a place where medical facilities are already inadequate due to conflict. I can't believe what is happening in our world! The news is all about human suffering - natural disasters, the ongoing war in Ukraine, murders: and in the UK, strikes by NHS and other workers.

I can't eat my meal, and struggle to get anything down. I have to force myself, because I can't take my tablets without food. Then, to my horror, I vomit up the tiny amount I have eaten. I don't take the tablets. I'm afraid. I feel weak and wonder what is happening. For the rest of the evening I have only water. Thank goodness, this drip session is week three, with the fourth as a 'rest' week.

7th February

I have had a restful night, without further sickness, and to my relief, manage to eat some porridge and take my tablets. I text my granddaughter to wish her a happy sixteenth birthday. It's a day of feeling tired and sorry for myself again.

8th February

I awake feeling scared and confused. Today is preparation for tomorrow's colonoscopy. The leaflet of how and when to take this stuff that empties your bowels is so confusing. I eat very little all day, but force myself to take the stuff at 7.30pm (Moviprep Orange). I manage to get it down but vomit some back up. By about 9.30pm the movements begin and I rush to the toilet. Speed is important! Thank goodness for those thick padded pants - though I feel like a baby wearing a nappy. As the night wears on, I get up multiple times to empty myself, and by morning am exhausted. But the job is done. Surely I am 'empty' enough.

9th February
We set off to Salford Royal for the dreaded procedure. I sit in the chair, waiting to go in, when a strange feeling comes over me, as if I am about to faint. Two nurses lead me onto a bed in a tiny ante room, and call the doctor to see if I am well enough to undergo the procedure. He thinks I am dehydrated, so they put me on a fluid drip. Thankfully I can have the procedure - and I want to get it over with. Apparently my prep has not been thorough enough, so they can't see as much as they hoped. I am sedated, via oxygen through tubes in the nose. To my intense relief, the actual procedure is nowhere near as bad as I had anticipated. I relax and let it happen. If I have to undergo this again, I intend to get precise instructions on how to take my day-before prep.

I doze on the sofa for the rest of the afternoon. I can't eat my meal of salmon and veg, and worry about my body's lack of nutrients. I manage to eat a small rice pudding and nibble a few grapes, which thankfully I don't vomit back up.

I read through a copy of the report they will send to my doctor, but it might as well be written in Chinese.

10th February
Here we are again - another day of tablets and rest. I decide to take my final six chemo tablets, then rest until my second cycle (20th). I think about whether these symptoms are 'normal' - extreme tiredness, urine infrequent and darker than usual, frequent burping, loss of appetite, so eating only tiny amounts, minor nose bleeds, sore mouth and itching. I feel like I've been drugged. I suppose I have, as the cancer nurse did describe the chemo tablets as 'poison'. My daughter assures me that the 'rest' week should help me recover my energies. I hope she's right.

Paige, my eldest granddaughter rings. We have a lovely chat, about her job and how well she is doing. She laughs when I describe her as a 'go-getter.' But she is, and I am so proud of her achievements. She is happy!

11th February

I wake up feeling positive. No more tablets until the 20th! Time to get things done. So I make a time plan for between now and when the chemo will be finished - the first week in July, thinking that the more I can look forward to a revamped home, the better I will feel.

The decorator is due on Monday to start the bedroom, as well as the man who is repainting the front paintwork outside. It's a start.

My partner and I have a row about the house, and needing to change things. Harsh words are said and we are like prickly hedgehogs. Later he goes shopping and returns with some Valentine roses - a truce of sorts. I am so emotional about everything, tears fall.

12th February

Sunday: C, my partner, brings me a cup of tea in bed, with a banana. We talk a little, and I explain what 'hope' means to me now. This illness has forced change, whether we like it or not - move forward into a new chapter or stay as we are. By July I will know which way this cancer treatment is going. I explain why moving forward is so important to me: that 'hope' means something light, bright and new, as we move out of this dark tunnel. If I survive this, and live, then I must try to feel happy. So we agree to use my chemo cycles positively as moving on points. Weeks 4 (rest) and 1 are my best for doing stuff, meeting up with friends and moving my writing on, while weeks 2 and 3, as the chemo tablets kick in, will be utterly useless. So this is the pattern. I have written these dates in my diary so that we can plan each small step. Meanwhile, as we update each room of our home, and declutter at the same time, I have devised a decision-making chart. Is each item for: *Use, Ornament, Repair, Or Rubbish?* Simple questions that we can hopefully answer together as we move forward.

The family arrive about 2.00pm: party day for Marcia's 16th birthday. It's such a lovely get together: a full afternoon of love and laughter. I don't do anything, just sit and join in. Tracey brings me some nutrient sachets. So thoughtful, plus a bracelet for my nausea issues. I revel in the happy company and forget my health problems for the rest of the day.

13th February

Up early for the decorator. The house will be a mess for three days, but it's a start. One room at a time. Onward and upward! My friend, Judith, phones for a chat. Not much writing gets done in the morning. I end up having a long chat with two other friends, one of whom is also on his cancer journey. We share our experiences. Not exactly uplifting but it helps to talk. Then I tutor Nat on his maths. All in all a day of chatting and doing - but no writing.

14th February
Valentine's Day! I give my partner his card. Then I book my next 'bloods session' for the 17th. I get lots of writing done (Chapter 2 of my Memoir, and Chapter 12 of novel) and manage to feel some sense of achievement.

15th February
The decorator is almost finished. I have lunch with my friends Judith and Christine, then attend my writing group. I realise how important it is to carry on doing things, meeting people and talking about stuff that matters to me. I begin Chapter 3 of Memoir, and end the day content.

16th February
It's my art class this morning. I've decided to attend each month on 'rest' weeks, so must make the most of it. I enjoy painting my watercolour of an orangutan climbing a tree in the jungle. Maybe it will inspire me to start on the 'Paint by Numbers' of my grandchildren that Tracey got me for Christmas 2021. I know that getting back to my art will help me through this dark tunnel.

We sort out the bedroom that the decorator has just completed painting. I love the colours, and await our new curtains. Much brighter! I am determined to bring light and colour into our home. These 'house' goals are important markers, helping me to move forward. Room number one 'decluttered.' Next step - conservatory!

To my surprise, I receive a phone call at 4.45pm from my Christie's doctor, asking me how it's going. Apparently I should have received a letter about this, but haven't. I feel comforted to know that this phone call will be monthly and that I will have regular opportunities to ask questions as this treatment continues.

17th February
Bloods day. My 'rest' week is almost over and I dread the start of a new cycle. I spend the morning writing/editing my three projects, and feel pleased with myself. Lunch at Costa (again!). Food shopping - hardly exciting. But, I get through the day. That's positive!

18th February

Saturday: we go out to look for new stuff for the house: brighter lamp shades, rug, cabinet, linen basket, etc. No brown allowed! We return only with a new pillow and some light shades. Every little helps, as they say. I exchange a Christmas book token at Waterstones - four new novels to help me escape reality. During the evening I am so tired I doze on the sofa.

A letter arrives from Christie's- apparently the phone call I received Thursday was because they are not having consultations face to face, due to the Virus. Virus! Please, please don't tell me this is rearing its ugly head again! As if the NHS has not got enough problems.

19th February

Sunday: both daughters are meant to be coming round for the usual scrabble game, and get together. But my younger one rings to say she has a bad cold and doesn't want to risk me catching it, as with my immune system being low, it could badly affect my reaction to the chemo. So we arrange to meet next week. I look forward to my elder one's company, and we end up having the most wonderful chat, partly because it's not often I see Debbie one-to-one. We end up telling each other stuff that we have never aired before and share memories that surprise each of us - a warm, lovely and relaxing afternoon. How lucky I am to have such a beautiful relationship with both my daughters, whom I love so dearly.

As part of my decluttering programme, I sort out jewellery that I will never wear again, to offer my girls. Amongst these, are pieces that belonged to my mother. I finger her wedding ring and try it on - a strange feeling comes over me, as if she is watching. Then her engagement ring, with a dark red stone, that was always covered in flour when she baked. I pack the assortment of brooches, rings, bracelets and necklaces back into the box and place them in a drawer.

20th February

Cycle 2 begins with the 9.30 drip session. I ask to change the time to afternoon, so that Chris can still go to his football. The nurse explains why the time cannot always be the same, as different drip sessions need to be fitted together like a jigsaw - some sessions last five hours! Imagine! I feel okay after my half hour drip. I am to start the tablets from tomorrow. The rest of the day is writing - my C diary, memoir and novel. I remind myself that this week's house goal is to declutter my 'office', and get old rockers, inherited from my parents, to the charity shop. I feel a slight pang as he

38

carries them out to the car. Yet, common sense tells me that they have had their day.

The doctor rings in the afternoon, just for a 'how are you' update. She'll ring again in a month. Tiredness descends again. From about 3.00pm I'm fit for nothing, so lie on the sofa to read, doze or watch telly.

21st February

I book my bloods for this Friday, 24th at 1.40. Done! What a relief. Then I stare at the chemo tablets, hating them, yet knowing I have to begin this second cycle. I remind myself that they are 'good', even if they will make me feel rotten. Must drink more water! The day passes. Nothing goes wrong. Yet, nothing is right. It's just a day.

22nd February

I start today with a positive statement, and write it in my daily book: I WILL get the best from my day! Morning is writing. Afternoon is my writers' meeting. We have a good, interactive meeting talking about what is wrong with the world, as well as writing. It's good to talk and air my views. I worry a lot about what is happening in our world today. Instead of fighting natural disasters (such as climate change) some people prefer to fight other humans. I really don't get it.

23rd February

I have the day to myself, so must make the most of my energies. I have a short walk, then get stuck in to my writing. My memoir helps lift my thoughts from present darkness. Who will read it? Anyone? Is this exercise a mere cleansing of my mind - or an examination of my thoughts, leading on to my final life-changing choice? I have come to the conclusion that pure happiness is not for me. Too many regrets and dark thoughts haunt me daily. Yet, I may still find peace and contentment. Are my memoirs helping me work towards this final stage of life, and decision making?

Time passes - nothing goes wrong, yet nothing is right!

24th February

It's bloods day, then Costa for lunch. This afternoon we pick my granddaughters up from school and spend precious time with them. How I have missed their childish silliness! My elder one (16), is stressed about her forthcoming GCSE's. They are doing 'mocks', and her higher maths paper stresses her out. The younger (10) is preparing for her Year 6 SATs - much of which is problem solving and reasoning. They will both succeed! I know it. We have fish and chips from the chippie, and I am freed from my own problems for a little while.

Today is the first anniversary of the war in Ukraine. I hear refugees on TV talking about their experiences. Is there no end to human misery and Putin's pointless pursuit of power and control? There is no end in sight. Humans will continue to die unnecessarily, because of one insane man. How can this be?

25th February
Saturday: The decorator comes to finish the outside painting. It looks good. I work on my memoir, then we go off to the Trafford Centre to have a look around, as part of our house revamp. I manage to eat a delicious soup for lunch at John Lewis, and we get some ideas for the house as we wander. Then I have to get home. Tiredness overtakes me, as I walk, and sink gratefully into the car. The rest of the day is spent on the sofa. I watch 'Casualty' on TV as usual. A patient is told that her CT scan has shown up a mass on her pancreas, so she will need a biopsy. She bursts into tears. As I watch, fiction becomes reality and my own tears fall also.

26th February
A night of thinking between bouts of sleep. A poem about time rumbles around my brain, but I can't get it together: time, count, amount, minutes, hours, days - remind me how important it is not to waste the precious time we have. So today I make a timed list, intending to make the most of my day.

The family come round and we play Cluedo. It's fun and it gives me a lift. I am tired after all that activity.

27th February
It's week 2 of the treatment: 10.30. I dread it, but manage okay, glad that my drip session is only half an hour. Yet it seems longer as I wait, listening to the rhythmic hum of the machine and willing it to announce its final 'beep...beep'. The cancer nurse reminds me to drink more water. But as the day goes on tiredness overwhelms me. Write ...sleep ...write ...sleep. More sorting and decluttering. Then I manage to tutor Nat for one hour. After that, it's sleep time again.

28th February

Where has the month gone? I force myself to get up, wash and dress, but it's an effort. I manage only half of my healthy breakfast - of porridge, seeds and fruit. Even my writing is hard and I have to force myself. Focus! Don't give in to this urge to lie down and doze.

But I do give in. It's a day of feeling sorry for myself. I lie on the sofa, watching the new film 'All Quiet on the Western Front' - the horrors of 1917-18. How those men suffered! I would have liked more in the film about the story of the war - how and why it happened? It was so graphic, yet communicated the utter senselessness - 17 million dead, and millions more left with life changing injuries. Yet only 21 years later the second war? Senseless! I think again about the war In Ukraine, and my own problems disappear for a short while.

1st March

I awake with determination to move forward with decluttering while my energy is at its best, and feel pleased with myself. New month! New start to dealing with this 'thing'. If those WW1 soldiers could launch themselves into battle with courage, then so can I.

I start the day with Complan, thinking the more nutrients I can force into this weak body, the more weapons I have to fight with. It's vanilla, and I manage to get it down. Well done! It's the writers' meeting this afternoon, but only four of us. Not much writing. But it's nice to talk about anything. I read out part of my memoir. Then I rest, exhausted.

2nd March

I start with a house cleaning task, thinking I'll get it done while my energy is here, and feel pleased with my efforts.

My Creon tablets arrive in the post - thank goodness. I was afraid of running out. I receive an email about Corona virus - it seems I am now in that vulnerable category of people with medical conditions. It worries me that this virus is still with us, and also, how vulnerable I am to catching it, or any illness, as my immune system is so low.

My partner's car has a problem so we go out in mine, but we have a huge row because he finds fault with everything - the seat is too far forward, he doesn't like the mat on the floor. He calls my car a 'shed' because there is stuff stored in it. I burst into tears. It feels like the end of the world, and the sobs won't stop. We don't speak for the rest of the day and evening. I can't look at him. I feel myself retreating.

The highlight of my day is seeing my grandchildren: listening to their silly chatter and talking with my daughter, who is feeling frustrated, having to wait a whole month (24.3) for the results of her latest scan. I empathise with her worries: her journey has gone on for almost nine years. Yet, she is still with us: a wonderful testament to our NHS. She too has received her letter about the virus, so is still in the vulnerable category. Our lovely family time warms my heart a little.

3rd March
Bloods day: 1.40. I awake determined to have a good day, so write affirmations: I WILL have a positive day! I WILL move forward! I WILL find peace! Then I think about what 'peace' actually means. For me, it refers to that inner quiet, contentment and above all, <u>acceptance</u>, that enables me to think that all is well in my life. A poem begins to form in my head but I can't get the words together: soft, gentle, silky, roses, yellow, pink, light, glow - lovely words that conjure up that feeling of warmth and inner peace. The words float around my brain, but don't seem to connect. I can't force it. All my poems come from my head, as and when *they* are ready.

After the bloods, we go to Costa for lunch, but I can't eat much. I stare around the coffee shop. Tears are not far away. He makes small talk but I am still unable to respond. He apologises for yesterday - then the tears flow again. Suddenly I know what is wrong. The feeling is so familiar - an emptiness as if nothing matters any more. I don't want people. I don't want anything. I don't want to be seen or touched. Have I sunk again into that dark and lonely place I know only too well, having had two previous emotional breakdowns, one in 1988, the second around 2016? I don't want depression tablets again. Nor do I want counselling. I WILL sort myself out.

4th March
Saturday, a new day, and a fresh start! A strange question occurs to me. Is my emotional pain now stronger and more debilitating than the physical discomfort from cancer? Are they emanating from the same source - each affecting the other? Has my emotional pain got the power to limit my recovery - IF I let it? Yes, probably. So, I WILL NOT let it. Somehow, I will climb out of this dark place and into the light. My goal is to live for a further 7 years - to the age of 85. And those seven years CAN be happier. I will make them happier. I will die, at the very least, content and at peace with myself!

5th March: Sunday

This date is the anniversary of my first marriage in 1966 - that went so disastrously wrong, and influenced my life for many years. This relationship, one of four significant 'men' relationships, features in the memoir I am working on, as a key crisis. Yet, it's just a date! 57 years ago. In the past - long since dead, like the man himself.

My younger daughter pops over for scrabble and knitting, and brings the fold up piano. She sets up my 'painting by numbers kit', but we need a magnifying glass to see some of the tiny numbers. We have a delightful day, as usual.

I am panicking, having lost my 'copy and paste' facility on the iPad. So she just turns off the device, turns it on again, and hey presto, the CP is working again.

I have so many projects, I can't think how I am going to keep them moving: writing, painting, knitting, decluttering rooms, and learning to play two carols on the piano by Christmas! Wow!

My partner makes the three of us a chilli for dinner, but it's so spicy, it burns my mouth, and I can't eat it. So I have some Complan instead. The children arrive, dropped off by their Dad, as it's been his weekend to have them. More silly chatter - I smile. It's been a good day.

6th March

Chemo day: 1.00pm - week 3. I am prepared for a bad week. To my amazement, a magnifying glass arrives at 9.00 - as if by magic. Can't believe the speed of online ordering and delivery - thank you, Tracey! I will finish number 16 on my painting today!

I feel woozy as I wait for the treatment, as if I'm about to faint. I tell the nurse and she reacts quickly, raising my feet and letting me lie down. It seems my blood pressure has dropped. All is back to normal in a minute or so, and I have the treatment. I spend the rest of the day dozing on the sofa again, completely wiped out. Painting? No way! I can't even eat my meal, and vomit up what bit I manage.

7th March

It's Complan for breakfast - can't face anything else. I doze on the sofa for a while. It's one of those days when I can do nothing. Not even writing!

My friend Judith phones me with update and queries on my novel that she is editing and proofing. It's wonderful - she has almost reached the end, and has given a copy to another writing friend, who says she is enjoying reading it. She even suggests a better title, 'A Lie Never Dies.' What a relief! I trust Judith so much, and feel thankful that she has taken on the job for me. So I may just end up with a completed novel by early summer - a chink of light in my darkness. Meanwhile, I have to work on the blurb and think about the cover, and acknowledgments.

But, for the rest of the day and evening, I can only lie on the sofa and watch TV. I feel a little sorry for myself.

8th March
This morning I have a normal bowel movement, manage some porridge and feel just a teeny, weeny bit more lively than yesterday. I hold my bottle of holy water and pray to our Lady - asking for help and strength. So let's make this a good day. I manage to work on my memoir for an hour or so.

My elder daughter, Debbie, rings and we have a lovely long chat. She cheers me up. Then it's downhill - lying on the sofa again. No painting done! No knitting! My positivity deserts me for a while, as I feel so lousy. It's as if normal life has ceased. I imagine what it must be like to live your whole life in such a weak state, as many sick and disabled people do. It's no good feeling sorry for myself.

9th March
I feel much the same, but remind myself it is the dreaded 'week 3'. It takes all my energy to shower and dress. I make my list of things to do - including my painting. If I can manage it today I will feel much better. I don't manage it. I lie and doze on the sofa all day.

10th March
Up early for my 9.20 am appointment at Wythenshawe hospital, although we have no idea what it is for. It has been snowing, a freak return of winter weather. We set off at 8.00 to allow for traffic, and arrive in plenty of time. We wait, and after half an hour, the consultant finally arrives and informs me that we did not need the appointment after all. What a waste of time! I had been sitting there, dreading awful news about my liver. The consultant says I don't look jaundiced, so at least that is positive, in spite of the wasted journey.

We arrive home. I take my tablets and try to settle down. In the post there is a letter from Salford Royal about my colonoscopy: a copy of that sent from the Salford consultant to the Christie, therefore riddled with medical terminology. I read it a few times and heave a sigh of relief at the words I can make sense of - *'no evidence of colorectal cancer was identified…. a 4-5 cm laterally spreading tumour … a benign lesion …low grade dysplasia… additional benign adenomatous polyp … 13 mm in the rectum'*. I take heart from the words 'benign'. For weeks I have been expecting dire news from the results of the colonoscopy on the 9th February. Having been told I had two cancers had placed huge fear in my heart. This news is good - one cancer instead of two! But I collapse in floods of tears. Relief overwhelms me! It seems all I now have to deal with is the pancreatic.

Also in the post this morning are some Covid tests, as I am in that vulnerable category. So good news today - inspiring me to pull myself together and get rid of negative imaginings. I CAN and WILL get through this!! So, let's get on - writing, painting, knitting?

And I do! I actually do some painting, and knitting. And feel satisfaction from it.

11th March

Saturday: I wake up feeling positive - ready to move forward. It's a bright day, and the snow has gone where we are. I make my list of jobs. I manage to write a bit - this diary and my memoir, and even research 'Titanic staterooms', to give additional depth to the final chapter of my historical novel, as suggested by Judith.

But then the day dips and my energies fade, along with the sunshine. I can hardly eat, my strength plummets and I end up on the sofa again. Even standing is an effort. Is this a catch 22: the tablets preventing me from eating, while not eating is worsening their side effects? I don't know, but can't force food down if it makes me feel sick. I also have stomach pains, with attacks of diarrhoea today.

So I give in. Watch TV and sleep. Keep calm and carry on. No painting! No knitting! 'Tomorrow is another day', as Scarlett O'Hara famously said.

12th March

It's family day and I'm looking forward to it, but hope I can last out until the evening. I write a bit, then manage to tidy up and get ready for their arrival. What a wonderful afternoon we have! It lifts my heart to hear us all chatting and laughing. I even manage to work on a 'ratio' maths problem with my granddaughter, in Year 6, practising for her SATS this summer. She struggles to apply her excellent mathematical knowledge to the reasoning and problem solving aspect of the subject, so we share a chocolate bar into

45

different ratio parts, then enjoy eating it. My elder daughter, Debbie, sorts me out with 'Linked-in' on my iPad, in order to help market my latest educational book. We also get out the family photos and sort through them, trying to identify long gone relatives. The girls have fun and laugh at what their mum, Debbie and me looked like when we were younger. A positive day all round. I manage to forget my problems.

13th March

No chemo! It's 'rest' week. And the final day of my chemo tablets. Hurrah! But I wake up feeling quite woozy and weak: even struggling to wash and dress. There's nothing I can do about it. I have learned that it's no good fighting this - so I work with it and lie on the sofa for a while until I can rouse myself. But that woozy feeling hangs around all day. I take my final tablet for this second cycle at 10.30 pm. That's it for a whole week.
Tracey phones and we have a lovely chat. And my friend, Judith, phones - she has flu. What a day! I agree to read her novel before she sends it for publication.

14th March

I wake up feeling just as bad as yesterday. I had planned to meet a friend for lunch tomorrow, but it's not going to happen. I also cancel my planned art session on Thursday. No tablets today, and for a whole week. Not much happens. I watch Endeavour on TV. Try to read a bit. I'm worried about eating - this catch 22 again. If I can't eat, I have no energy, yet I have no energy to eat. I manage six glasses of water - the goal is eight. I remind myself to make a list of these problems for when the consultant rings on Thursday.

The news is sad again - the worst tropical storm ever in Malawi, with thousands homeless, and injured. People are buried in the mud. Is there no end to the natural disasters of our world? Later, I watch an episode of 'Grace' on TV - a gruesome plot involving the dark web, and people who kill and sell body parts for the gratification of others who revel in death. Death for entertainment? Such a level of human depravity sickens me. I remind myself that it's only fiction. Yet, is not fiction built upon human experience and knowledge of what some humans are capable of?

15th March

What a delightful start to the day! Marcia, my sixteen year old granddaughter rings me with the results of her mocks. She sounds ecstatic

- a range of grades - five for maths, but eight for English language and literacy, some sixes and sevens, and a distinction star! As she says, much to build on, but so positive. Wow! I am so pleased for her, and the fact that she has phoned me at 8.55 am, just to tell me, warms my heart so much.

I listen to a programme on the radio about the benefits of 'expressive writing'. A research study points to the value of writing about our bad experiences, to get them out of our heads. I testify to this as I have been doing it for years, and still am. Even writing these daily extracts helps me cope with what is happening.

I write down my goals for the day. Can I paint a little? No. As the day progresses, it's obvious that all I can do is lie down. So I give in.

16th March

I want the clock to stop and the night to never end. Night is normal. All I have to do is lie down. Day is not normal because I can't do what I want to do. But time moves on relentless. I manage a shower, some porridge - pray for energy and begin another day. I make a list of what I will say to the doctor when he phones for his monthly check up on me: intense lethargy, not eating, continual burping and stomach pains. Is the stent working effectively, and not blocked from 'debris'? I also want to ask him about the letter from Salford, suggesting that the lumps observed from the colonoscopy are 'benign' and nothing to worry about.

The consultant phones about 4.30 and reassures me on the above points: they are side effects but not dangerous. He tells me that the bloods should identify any problem with the stent, but that I am not taking enough Creon tablets, the enzymes that help my food (what little there is) to be effectively digested, so I resolve to take more. He also tells me that the benign polyps in my rectum could turn cancerous if left too long (years?) and therefore should be removed at some point. All in all, I end our conversation feeling a little reassured. Keep calm and carry on.

My friend, and writing colleague, Judith, rings and offers to rework the final chapter of my 'Lie' novel for me. I am so grateful, as I don't have the mental energy. I have agreed to read and critique her novel. It's great that we are collaborating.

I do little except read and doze. How much sleep does one body need? I assume this excessive tiredness is from not eating, so for dinner I attempt egg, chips and peas, with more Creon tablets. I am doing well - until suddenly I rush to the loo and vomit my egg and chips back up. I stare at the undigested bits of egg white floating in the toilet bowl and can't understand why. But there's no point in getting upset or angry. I will try again tomorrow. No painting today either!

17th March

I think about my goals as I lie in bed, determined to have a better day. I am not going to achieve everything I have set out to do - time now will not allow it, and many writing projects partly done, will likely remain unfinished. But maybe I can achieve *some*. Here they are, for 2023:

Media and marketing	Writing/publishing	Other Creative pursuits
Learn to understand and take control of book marketing: my website, PayPal, linked in, Instagram etc. Continue blogging	Self publish my 'Lie' novel Publish memoirs Publish this diary of my cancer journey	Painting - finish painting by numbers Resume personal artwork Finish knitting project Learn to play a simple Carol on the piano for Christmas 2023!

There seems no point in making longer term plans. I will focus on the here and now.

I am fearful of eating but make some Complan and manage to get all of it down - with more Creon tablets - so far, so good.

It's bloods day - 1.40 pm. I have developed a psychological fear of the treatment clinic, and feel panic as I walk, holding onto my partner's arm, into the building. But it takes only minutes. Then it's Costa for lunch, but I can't eat much, just a slice of cake. Then home again - TV, doze and read. Another day gone.

18th March

Saturday: I try again to focus on moving forward. Complan for breakfast. I remember to take more Creon with it, and to my relief it stays down. Then it's writing again. Suddenly I rush to the loo - only just in time. I wasn't prepared for this attack of diarrhoea.

I force myself to go to the carpet shop to look at some Amtico covering for our scruffy porch - as part of our house improvement programme. We make an appointment for the fitter to come and look at the job. One small step at a time! I feel exhausted, having walked from the car to the shop and back. I recall the time when we regularly enjoyed meals out in Monton, a village not far from where we live. I can't imagine going to a restaurant ever again. We don't even stop for a coffee because I can't manage it.

I'm desperate to get home - doze, rest and watch TV. Nothing changes.

19th March

Mothers' Day! The day begins with an urgent visit to the loo. My poo is much paler than usual and I make a mental note to mention this to the nurse tomorrow. It's writing as usual - I've reached the part of my memoirs that speculates on my future, as an achiever and as a writer. Do I still have the time to achieve what I want to do? My future seems so open-ended, I'm not sure who or what is in control - me or IT? Can my positivity actually influence the outcome?

The family arrive - what joy. Flowers and chocolates, and delightful messages from the girls on my 'To Grandma on Mother's Day' card. The girls have given their mum a key ring, heart shaped, with a photo of the three of them inside. Tracey does some of my painting by numbers for me, and I help the youngest with her maths reasoning questions - line graphs. We play scrabble. By 8.30 I feel exhausted, but gaze at the flowers on my mantel piece and think how lucky I am.

20th March

Treatment day - it begins with a strange poo, like a coiled length of beige-coloured rope. But I feel okay. I text my friend to say that I will try to tutor her son, Nat, later today. Fingers crossed!

My friend, Judith, has reworked the last chapter of my novel, so I need to read it. I also need to continue reading hers. I start my writing as usual, then my partner takes me for the treatment. Cycle three, out of six. A new nurse, Dave, with a lovely bedside manner, directs me to the chair, asks me how I am, and discusses my symptoms with me. All seems okay - getting through this is all about nutrition, and water, water, water. I must try harder with the water. The treatment is okay, but I am tired and need to go straight home. Dave has booked my next bloods for Friday, so that's done.

Later, I manage to tutor Nat for an hour on his maths, and feel pleased

49

with myself. But back home, I start to shiver, and have to huddle beneath a blanket. I don't know if it's just cold, or the effect of the treatment, but the shivering lasts a while. Dr. Green from the surgery rings. I explain about the pale poo, and she mentions the possibility of jaundice. Fear grips me. She says she will send an email to my Christie consultant about this. It's another evening watching TV and dozing.

21st March
Okay so far, but something tells me that today will be a wipe out. The pale stools have ceased, thank goodness, and I'm not shivering. It's the first of my new cycle of chemo tablets, so I get them over with and try to write.

My friend, and writing colleague, Judith, rings and we discuss both our novels - very productive. I must do the blurb and acknowledgements. Then I read the next part of her novel.

Tracey rings with the results of her scan: all clear! Hallelujah! She doesn't like her new oncologist, but it's the message that matters. She will have a further scan in three months. But it's now time to let go and move her life forward, after her nine year cancer journey. I encourage her to book for a weekend in New York with her friends. She needs it.

Then I doze again and let the rest of the day float by.

22nd March
Wednesday: I want to go to the writers' meeting today. I write as usual, and attend the meeting. It does me good to socialise and talk about different aspects of writing. Bill, in our group, is about to format my first novel and obtain a proof copy. I'm quite excited! All that talking and socialising has drained me. It's dozing time again.

At dinner I vomit up the egg again. I don't understand why. I ate some quiche okay and there is egg in that. Is it the olive oil from frying? It's disappointing. But no more fried eggs!

23rd March
Here we are again. I try to put some positivity into myself as I wash and dress, and start my day with Complan - 26 nutrients. Great! I manage a first draft of the 'blurb' for the back cover of my historical novel. It takes a while to get all the key strands together, with enough mystery to entice readers. Then I settle down to read a section of Judith's novel, and admire her ability to bring WW2 back to life through the dialogue and actions of her characters. She is much better at 'painting word pictures' through

characterisation than I am.

For lunch I manage to eat two whole crumpets with cottage cheese on. That's a bonus.

In the afternoon, my partner drives me over to see my other writing friend, Jean, whose granddaughter would like a copy of my latest educational book (The SENCO Survival Guide, published by Routledge, 2022). She is writing her university dissertation on SEND, so I am delighted to give her a copy. Jean and I spend a delightful hour chatting about our projects - until I feel my eyes start to droop, and my body tells me I must come home. But at least I've been out. I sleep for two hours again.

Later, I manage to eat a tiny amount of fish, about four chips and one spoonful of peas, enough to satisfy a small child. Before bed, I try some fruit and enjoy the taste of pineapple and blackberries for a change - but minutes later, I vomit it back up. Is it the citrus? Is fruit now something else I cannot digest? I seem to be running out of foods I enjoy, and can also keep down.

24th March

What will this day bring? Probably much the same. My days are falling into a pattern. It starts with one of my very pale poos - not quite diarrhoea, but very loose. I write as usual, and even do one row of knitting, then attend my 'bloods' session. The nurse on duty takes one look at me and suggests that we need to halt the IV treatments for a week. My weakness is worse than it should be in her view. We discuss my inability to eat, apart from the Complan. She encourages me to try energy foods - to put sugar in my tea (Ugh!). At Costa I manage only half a slice of cake, then have to get home and rest. Then the usual - TV and doze. Nothing changes.

25th March

Another pale poo. Is it because I am mainly drinking Complan? I write as usual. My friend Bill rings to ask if he can come over for me to choose a cover for my historical novel, but I haven't got the energy, so I ask him to choose a temporary cover for the proof copy, to be changed later.

Amongst the post is a letter, with an appointment at Christie's for 13th April. I make a mental note to tell the consultant how washed out I feel, physically and mentally, about the poos, sickness - and the latest symptom, a pain in my right calf. Do I need a reduced dosage? Is the stent blocked up? It's hard to imagine existing in this state until July!

I wait all day for the phone call from the nurse, to tell me if I have to still take the tablets, even if the IV is on temporary hold for a week. The phone call does not come, so I take my tablets as usual. As the day goes on I can hardly stand, so I just sleep and read a bit. I must not give in to this. But it's hard to feel positive when I feel so low.

26th March

Sunday: a lie in, but we have lost an hour as the clocks go forward. I struggle to get dressed, and have to keep sitting down. The routine is the same - Complan, tablets, write, read - and, of course, doze on the sofa.

My daughter, Tracey, comes over in the afternoon. She does some of my painting by numbers for me, then we play scrabble. For the first time (with a little helpful prompting) I manage to equal her score. We have a lovely chat.

Chris cooks roast chicken for tea and I manage a roast potato and a tiny amount of veg - but, to my horror, I vomit it back up. I stare at it, floating in the toilet bowl - bits of carrot, red pepper, sprouts and potato, and feel despair. But there is nothing I can do.

Then the children arrive, dropped off by their dad. The youngest is off on a PGL break in the Lakes this week with her school. How lovely! Walking, canoeing, climbing! Oh, how I envy her energy and love of life.

Tracey has sad news for the children. Hooper, the hamster, has died. Marcia (16 and highly emotional) bursts into tears. So tomorrow, after work, they will bury him in a shoebox in the garden.

27th March

Am I imagining it - or do I have a little more energy this morning? I shower, dress, and feel a little brighter. I even walk better. Maybe that awful few days has passed. Fingers crossed. I can cope with this okay. The pain in my calf is not so bad. I feel calm and relaxed. The nurse rings about lunchtime to tell me not to take my chemo tablets this week. Hurray! A whole week free. Yet, common sense reminds me that I can't keep having weeks off - this treatment has a purpose. We ring John Lewis to organise a fitting day for our new rail and curtains - a small step for our house update.

Writing - a bit of my memoir, then I read the third section of my friend, Judith's, novel. In the afternoon I watch a captivating programme about the late artist, Frieda Kahlo, born in Mexico in 1907, who overcame numerous emotional and health challenges in her life, to achieve success. I admire her amazing strength and tenacity, her sense of purpose. Following a severe accident, when the bus in which she was travelling crashed, she even painted lying in her hospital bed. Her own creativity helped her through this, and further traumas. A message for us all. Above all this lady was an individualist who did her own thing and was not afraid to shock people through her extraordinary paintings. She died aged only 47 - but what a colourful and inspirational life she led!

28th March
Okay so far - pale poo again, but at least I'm going. I am again calm and relaxed and ready to create my day. Wow! No tablets. A good writing session in the morning. My friend, Judith, phones and we chat about our books: I feed back my thoughts on her novel structure, while she updates me on my forthcoming proof copy. Neither of us likes the chosen cover but that can be changed for the final copy. Then Veronica phones and we chat in general. Thirdly, my daughter, Debbie, rings and we have a cosy one-to-one. After all this talking I am exhausted and have to lie down. Odd how merely talking uses up mental energy. I relax and read more of my philosophy book by Nigel Warburton. Then it's TV and doze. Another day gone - one day nearer to the end of this journey.

29th March
I awake calm and relaxed again - my energy levels about the same as yesterday. Usual writing in the morning - the final paragraphs of my memoir - only first draft. How strange to complete this project even though my life has not yet reached its 'real' end, and may not for some years. Now the much harder work of editing and adding bits to it begins, but at only 39,000 words I can manage it. My friend, Christine, rings and we chat. Her partner has been fighting cancer for a while, so we share our thoughts and jolly each other along.

Then it's the writing group. A lovely discussion about all sorts, except writing. We discuss the artist, Frieda Kahlo, and I explain why she is now my symbol of who I want to be and what I want to achieve - that I will draw energy and courage from her - and not be afraid to state my views, however controversial. From my latest, 'rainbow' book, 'Time of the Virus', I then end up 'singing' my amended single verse for the much-outdated song, 'Land of Hope and Glory' from my book. Veronica buys a copy. I hope she finds it as thought-provoking as it is meant to be. I make a mental note to market this book much more. From now on I am *not* afraid to court controversy! When we get home I spend the next two hours reading my book - as a reader, not as the author. I feel proud of what I have written and wonder why I have not publicised this work previously. Why was I so afraid of my own words?

30th March
Thursday - I opted out of the Art group this morning but intend to try my painting by numbers later. My energies are about the same as yesterday, so fingers crossed. Today will be a day of 'doing'. And it is! I write as usual, and in the afternoon, manage to paint for two hours, while also watching the 'Celebrity Painting Challenge' on TV. I feel determined, when this journey is over, to fully revive my own painting and to explore myself through my art, as my heroine, Frieda Kahlo, did.

Then my eldest granddaughter, Paige, phones and we indulge in delightful chat. Her life appears wonderful - with a good, loving partner, and both of them have lucrative, satisfying careers. Then I read more of Judith's book and make a note of some queries. As the day wears on, my energies slump. But it has been a positive and productive day.

31st March
Friday: bloods day. The psychological fear grips, yet I know that 'rest' weeks have to be followed by the IV. The nurse tells me I look better than last week, so the rest must have done me good. It takes four attempts to get some blood. The nurse also tells me that as this goes on, the veins become smaller. I am tired afterwards, and spend the rest of the day lying - writing, reading. I am beginning to feel calm and accepting of my situation. There is little point in fighting it - I can only outwit it.

Sad news - my elder daughter has Covid and can't come near me or anyone for a few days. She feels awful, but, having had all her jabs, is not seriously ill. But she can't join us at the weekend.

1st April
Saturday. I put finishing touches to my memoir (first draft), then send the file to my writing friend, Judith, who has offered to read and proof it. Then, I actually do some painting. Great! I can't go out, but plenty of reading and watching TV. I am fascinated by a nature programme about young orangutans at their 'jungle school' in Borneo, and marvel at the inventive teaching strategies of their human carers: for example, teaching them how to use sticks as tools to get honey water out of holes, and using a pretend snake as a decoy to teach these animals about 'snake danger'. It appeared just like a human school, with a different curriculum. It has been a reasonable day, calm, relaxed, and my spirits remain high because I have

accepted what now is. I am almost halfway through this treatment - a bit like approaching the summit of a mountain, ready to slide down the other side. Onward and upward.

<u>2nd April</u>
Sunday: my younger daughter and the children are coming over today. There is always something strange and unnerving about ending a writing project, albeit only a first draft. Having typed the final words of my memoir, my head is (temporarily) empty and I need to fill it. For thirty five years my head has been inhabited by some kind of writing - stories, educational books, poems, to keep my brain ticking over. So, what now?

The girls arrive and I indulge myself in a happy afternoon with them; playing Cluedo, helping my granddaughter with her maths for SATS, and watching their silly dancing. What joy, and what energy they have! Then, I manage to eat the delicious 'Lamb Navarin' my partner has cooked for us, my most enjoyable meal for a while. I surprise even myself.

Then, to my amazement, a large box is delivered - flowers from my partner's brother and family down in London - beautiful pink tulips. I cry. It's so heartwarming to know people care and are rooting for me.

<u>3rd April</u>
I've messed up my treatment time. It should be 9.30, and for some reason, I have 2.00 in my diary. How have I done that? The nurse rings to ask where I am, and I apologise. I am normally an organised person, and wonder if this process is affecting my head? Thankfully, they fit me in at 2.00. The nurse talks to me about eating, and explains that Complan is not meant as a food substitute - but as a supplement. The treatment is okay, but once back home, having read a little, I feel the need for sleep and am out of it for the rest of the day. It is hard work dragging myself off the sofa and upstairs to bed. My legs feel weak and unsteady. I remind myself of the purpose of this treatment - that it is also killing off the enemy lurking inside of me. Then I switch off the light and revel in the darkness of night.

I have been thinking about my Will, and wondering whether it is right to leave it as it is, as the fortunes of one side of my family have recently changed considerably for the better. I am considering rebalancing my assets according to need rather than equal shares. Yet, this is so difficult. How do I reassure my whole family that though my Will represents variations in need - in no way does this practical variation according to need have anything to do with my equal love for each person? I love everyone equally! A letter about my (paid up) dignity funeral plan also arrived today. Do I want to change or add anything? I cannot even think about this, so just place it on a pile for later. I fall asleep pondering on these vexing, yet important, issues.

4th April

Tablets begin again - get used to it, I tell myself. Nothing much on today - just write, read and rest. I try to eat better and drink more water, as the nurse has advised. I am waiting anxiously for my 'bloods' time this coming Friday, as the nurse said they will contact me. It's Good Friday, so we have to travel to Christie's.

5th April

Wednesday - my writers' meeting. I manage to send the blog I drafted yesterday. Then settle down to read more of my friend, Judith's, novel. Yesterday, she emailed to say how gripped she was by my memoirs so far. Heartwarming, but is this because she knows me as a friend? Would these memoirs be as gripping, if I was a stranger? I also read and comment on a writing group member's poems, having agreed to read these on his behalf before they become published. Then it's prep for the meeting.

Back home by 4.30 and it's lounging on the sofa again - exhausted from the talking. Maybe one social occasion is all I can manage in a day.

6th April

I am still waiting anxiously for the hospital to ring with the time for my bloods tomorrow. I get on with my writing - and send the blurb, cover photos etc. to be added to my novel, for the next proof, to Bill, my amateur publisher. Then my partner manages to phone to book the bloods - 2.20 tomorrow. Done! We have to go to Christie's as it's a bank holiday. I cannot imagine what I would do without my writing tasks, unable to move far from my sofa. I think I would go mad with boredom.

In the afternoon I have tummy ache, with attacks of diarrhoea - more of those beige-coloured poos, like lengths of coiled rope. Weird! I hope it doesn't mean anything dreadful. But I feel better afterwards.

I settle down to read and analyse poems written by a member of my writing group, and also read more of Judith's novel. The rest of the day floats by with nothing significant.

7th April

Good Friday, but Bank holidays mean little to us now. Once retired, they simply interrupt things. I settle down to write before going for my bloods - all the way to Christie's. I look around the bathroom and worry that I haven't been able to clean for ages. The kitchen floor must be filthy too. Maybe I will mop it later?

I write my next blog - views on institutional racism, and what we mean by it, inspired by an article in the Times. I am appalled by recent revelations about racism in the Met Police Force, and other organisations. Institutional or social? Is there no end to the racism issue? I want to publicise my new UK flag showing multicoloured arms reaching out towards the globe, from my recent 'Time of the Virus' book. But of course I won't. How I wish I had the courage to go public and be a campaigner.

At Christie's, we have lunch in the M/S cafe, and I enjoy half a pack of three bean salad and some mango chunks. I bring the rest home. The outing has exhausted me. So it's just rest and TV again.

8th April

I awake more tired and woozy than usual. It takes me ages to get dressed because I have to keep sitting on the edge of the bed. I lose it and have a good cry. Then I pull myself together and think about people who live daily with disability - limbs missing, no sight or hearing, or those who cannot even move unaided. My partner makes me a Complan before he goes off to Old Trafford for the football. I can't seem to do anything but I must accept it. If I am lucky, this situation is temporary only. I am half way through this treatment.

I think about my Will. I may need to amend it and make a mental note to phone for an appointment. Just in case - I may be a little closer to the grim reaper than previously thought.

An envelope arrives from the charity, MFPA: Mouth and Foot Painting Artists. I marvel at the sheer determination of creating beautiful artwork by holding the brush in the mouth or foot. I have been buying their Xmas and birthday cards for years. Most of us take the use of our hands for granted - but imagine being without them. Yes, I am lucky!

9th April

Sunday: Tracey is coming over today. We play scrabble and have a lovely chat. We enjoy 'The Sound of Music' on TV and, of course, I cry through most of it. The girls are dropped off by their dad about 7.15 and the house is suddenly alive with their laughter and silliness. I look at my younger granddaughters and pray that I will live to see them grow up. A lovely family day.

10th April
It's IV day at Christie's. I feel afraid. I write first and even do four rows of knitting before we set off, as I know I won't feel like it afterwards. We have lunch first at the M/S cafe in Christie's - half a salad and a piece of watermelon. I will take the rest home. We are told that they are about an hour behind schedule, so I receive treatment at 3.00 instead of 2.00. The extra wait seems endless. The nurse is kind. She realises how nervous I am and reassures me.

Back home, I rest on the sofa. The effects of the IV soon kick in and all I can do is sleep. Later, in the evening, I start to shiver and feel cold in spite of the blanket over me. I feel sick and bring up some of my dinner of salad and fruit. I have to get to bed. But I can't eat, so can't take my evening tablets. But it can't be helped. The sickness prevents it. Maybe it won't matter for once.

11th April
Each day is a new day - I start off hopeful - write and read as usual. I am continuing with the school training booklet on reading and comprehension, and am pleased with it so far. Judith phones and we spend a whole hour chatting about writing. Then Chris's brother, Nigel, phones. Then my daughter Debbie. By the end of this talking, lovely and heartwarming as it all is, I feel exhausted from the effort. The hours pass slowly, watching TV and dozing as usual. But there has been no more nausea.

12th April
Wednesday - our writing meeting is cancelled, as a few of us can't make it. So I settle for a day of writing and reading again. I am pleased with myself, having written more of my 'reading' training booklet for the school to use in my absence. Then I read Judith's novel, and am so impressed by the research that must have gone into this absorbing tale set in WW2.

The news again is so sad - yet more scandal and discrimination, this time from inside the CBI organisation. Atrocious bombing of civilians, including children, by the military government in Myanmar. In Iran, even schoolgirls are being deliberately poisoned by gas, simply for not wearing the hijab. I despair of the bullying and cruelty, and wonder where our precious world is going next.

In the UK, a nation supposed to represent fairness and equality, a new report suggests that 29% of people have reported gender or racial discrimination in education and/or employment. <u>How can we make our world better?</u>

<u>13th April</u>
I get up feeling okay. But, after having struggled to wash and dress, feel lightheaded, as if I am about to faint. I get downstairs and flop onto the sofa, thinking my blood pressure must have dipped again. Thankfully, I feel okay after a few minutes - and settle down to my usual writing tasks.

I make a list of my side-effects for my appointment with the consultant at Christie's. But when we arrive, I struggle to walk along to the bloods area. I feel faint, and the bloods nurse suggests I need a chair. I then end up being wheeled by a porter back down to the consultancy area. So embarrassing. Once in the chair, waiting for my name to be called, I start to feel woozy again. Chris calls the nurse and I am taken into a consultancy room, where they lie me flat and lift my feet up. I start to feel better, as the blood pressure count rises again. The doctor checks my heart and lungs. No problems. She feels at my tummy and looks at my legs - all seems well. They take my blood pressure every twenty minutes.

Then comes the bombshell. It's a shock. She thinks I need a complete rest from my treatment as it is affecting me far more than it should. The outcome: no more IV or tablets until after the next scan on 30.4.23 - after which they will have a multi-disciplinary meeting to decide next steps, and consult again with me in May. A whole month without treatment. But the big question - has the chemo so far shrunk the tumour enough to have the op when I am strong enough? Or will more chemo be necessary? But whichever it is, I need to get my body back to strength in order to undergo either.

Back home, I lie on the sofa and rest. No more treatment until the second week in May, when I see the consultant for the scan results. It's a bit open ended, wondering what will happen next. A whole month without tablets is so wonderful - but meanwhile, what is this tumour doing to my body?

<u>14th April</u>
I get up and remind myself - no tablets! It's a busy day - first my writing, then reading J's novel and a writing group member's poems, and my philosophy book. About 3.00 the gas man comes to put new parts on the

boiler, and my daughter comes to show me how to use the blender she has bought me. This month, free from treatment, is my opportunity to build up nutrition and strength. She brings a chair into the kitchen so that I can sit and watch as she makes soup and smoothies. It's confusing. I think I'll need a second lesson. Debbie leaves about 8.00 and I watch a thriller on TV, then news, and bed. It's been a good, interactive day, but my energy levels are still at rock bottom.

15th April

Saturday - we decide to go out and see a film. But first my writing - have almost done the first draft of my reading training booklet for the school. We have lunch at Costa, then enjoy a film at the Lowry cinema (Air), about a risk-taking venture to promote the 'Air Jordan' basket ball shoes, that have made millions for Nike. I enjoy lounging in the comfy chairs with my feet raised, and manage not to fall asleep. Back home, I've lost it again. My energy plummets. I can't believe that one small outing can take so much out of me. But it's no tablets - so I will bounce back! I will!

16th April

I wake up, and start the day hardly able to get to the toilet. I have a crying session, trying to explain to my lovely partner, how awful I feel at being so dependent on him. I need him to take me to get photos for the cover of my novel - otherwise it's held up. I feel guilty. All my life I have been independent - needing to move forward and achieve. This cancer is like a huge brick wall in front of me - a barrier I can't surmount without constant help. It's so frustrating!

It's Sunday, and the family come round for a late Easter celebration. My daughters bring chocolate for the Easter egg hunt. We have fun together, as usual. But I feel whacked when they go about 8.00.

17th April

I start on a positive note - determined to eat well, drink at least six glasses of water, and be productive. Okay. I might even try a short walk. The day does not quite unfold as I expect. Writing in the morning as usual, then lunch at Costa, where I manage half a biscuit and some apple juice. Quick visit to the bank, then home again. I manage to finish Judith's novel and email my comments to her. I also finish the first draft of my reading booklet for the school. Then it's out for the count - dozing on the sofa again. I've cancelled my hour's tutoring session with Nat. I don't understand why my energy levels aren't bouncing back. Not enough water? Not enough food? Not enough exercise to get my muscles back into gear?

18th April

I start the day by writing, 'I WILL live for five more years' in my daily notebook. How I live matters less now than simply living. Having finished the first draft of my school reading booklet, I am 'between' writing projects again, yet not quite ready to edit my memoirs. I have been reading a 'Little History of Philosophy' by Nigel Warburton. Fascinating! An idea forms. Can I write down my own philosophical thoughts on humanity - what needs to change? And how might we achieve it? Have I the courage to say what I think, however controversial? Can anyone philosophise? Yes, I think they can. We all have minds designed to think. I decide to write some notes and see where it leads.

Later I try a short walk, and manage to get a few photos of a large house with a lake in front, for the cover of my 'Lie' novel. The day moves on as usual. I find myself wondering if every day for the rest of my life will be spent in this state? But it doesn't matter. I'll simply live, and accept it.

19th April

I awake with gusto. This will be a productive day. I am assailed by Bill's ideas for my cover, and that he has skimmed and proof-read my novel and located a few errors. But my mind can't cope. I don't have the mental energy to make these changes. It's Wednesday - our writers' meeting, and to my relief, Judith steps in and offers to see to Bill's proofing queries, and has also taken over the cover issues. Now I can sit back and await my second proof - let's hope it's okay.

My ideas about philosophy begin to take shape. And I also consider writing a piece about Swanwick, the writing venue I have been attending annually for 33 consecutive years. This wonderful place, which sparked and inspired my entire writing career, has now ended for me, so I will write a farewell piece for Writing Magazine. I also finish and send my blog, 'Maths to 18?' responding to the PM's intention to have all young people study maths up to 18. A good writing day!

Also a better eating day - more protein. I go to bed content and positive.

20th April

We have appointments with the solicitor at 3.00 for our Wills. It's a thorny and difficult subject - how to apportion money fairly in a way that conveys the message that each member of my family has been equally loved and cherished. The nurse from Christie's rings to see how I'm getting on, following my woozy episode last week, and I tell her that I'm slowly getting some energy back and eating a little better. How nice of her to check up on me. I get on with my philosophy notes, trying to form a structure for how such a book could work. I am eating better - increasing my protein with peanut butter, amongst other stuff. I have prawns and salad for tea, and manage an orange before bed.

21st April
How the days fly by. Judith rings and I tell her how delighted I am with the front cover for the 'Lie' novel, designed by her friend, Dave. I realise how calm and relaxed I have become. I am no longer worried about the future. This illness is making me think about life differently. What used to bother me doesn't any more - trivial issues have faded into insignificance. And that is good. My OCD is less acute. The house is a mess but I'm less bothered than normal. I feel calmer, more relaxed, and remember those lovely lyrics sung by Doris Day: "Whatever will be ...will be. ....The future's not ours to see. Que sera, sera." How true. We can never know what lurks around the corner as our next challenge.

I eat well - Complan to start, prunes, banana, prawns, nuts and raisins, crumpets with peanut butter, tomatoes, tuna pasta bake for dinner - followed by an orange. I am trying to eat good stuff that I can keep down.

It's a productive writing day - thinking about a sequel for my 'Lie' novel (that has been deliberately left open-ended) and my proposed philosophy book, and making notes. It's good to have ideas floating around my head again - preparing to take shape. My head will never be empty.

Yet, all this thinking has tired me out. About 6.30 I feel myself drifting into oblivion- both mind and body have had enough. It's 'lie on sofa' time again until bed.

22nd April
I can't believe it's already four and a half months since my symptoms began, and the diagnosis. How quickly I have become used to days that come and go with not much to mark them out. It's Saturday and we have no plans to go out so it's the usual - write, read, knit and rest. I watch the last two episodes of 'Redemption' on TV and find myself crying. Is this the test of a good drama, when characters become so real, you take their troubles and challenges into your own heart? I forget my own problems for a while. In

the evening I give in to the lethargy.

23rd April
Sunday - family day. Judith has sent me the final cover for my 'Lie' novel. Great. I notice two typos on the blurb and email her about these. But it's done at last!!! I can't wait for my second proof copy to hold!

About 3.00 the family arrive and the fun begins. I lounge on my sofa, listening to their silly chatter and realise how life for them is full of expectation and excitement - at the ages of 16 and almost 11. The elder one shows us her prom dress (that my daughter has agreed to alter slightly for her) and practises wearing her shoes. I stare in horror at the six inch potential ankle-breakers as she hobbles around. The younger one is tired, having had a sleepover the previous night - it's obvious that sleep featured very little. Once again I do little but observe what is going on around me and soak it all in. Most of my life is gone, but I intend to enjoy what I have left through them.

When they have gone, I flop down and watch TV - and smile. It's been a good day.

24th April
I get up feeling a little stronger. I will have a good day. I write the next section of my philosophy book - on what is meant by 'belief', finish editing Warren's poems, then send my thoughts to Bill, who will help with his self-publishing. Later in the afternoon, I tutor Nat, who is 17 and at college. He has cognitive learning difficulties and ADHD and I have tutored him since primary school. He is studying Level 2 (equivalent to GCSE) and as we work through the problems on the sample paper, I realise they're a step too far. The challenges are too great. I doubt, sadly, that he will ever be able to think his way along each stepping stone of these complex maths problems. Yet his arithmetical speed and knowledge is superb. I am surprised the college is putting him through this, as Level 1 is surely his limit. Why invite failure?

Later I experience some strange symptoms - coldness and shivering, even though I have a blanket over me. By bedtime I can hardly climb the stairs, and flop into bed without even washing. Why have my energy levels dropped so low?

25th April
The man comes to fit our new rail and curtains. I love the material and pattern. But they have made the ones in the lounge far too short, so they

have to be remade. Two steps forward, one step back, as they say.

I settle down to write a bit of my philosophy book, until the phone calls begin - firstly my friend Dette, then granddaughter Paige, then Tracey, who is upset following a massive row with daughter Marcia (16) the previous evening. I try to reassure her it's just teenage angst and hormones, and remind her of our own mother and daughter arguments. At the end of the day, it's love that matters, and I reassure Tracey that whatever has been said, that mother/daughter love will always shine through. It's comforting to know that people who love me are out there, helping me along this strange journey.

In the evening we watch the final episodes of 'Blue Lights' on TV. The series has presented a different aspect to policing, focusing on first responders. Set in Belfast, it highlights the huge dangers police officers face when responding to violence on city streets. It's been an interesting day.

26th April

Wednesday - our writers' meeting. I look to see if anyone has written anything to be critiqued. There's just one piece from Veronica. Then I focus on the next section of my philosophy book - Freedom or the rule of law? I wonder whether anyone would want to read such thoughts? Why am I bothering? Do I have a strange mind? Maybe I am writing this to explore myself and what I truly think, and to encourage others to think deeply about issues around which humanity revolves - and evolves. Are we the 'subjects' of our own lives - or merely 'objects'? Mmm?

At the meeting we discuss differences between poetry and other types of writing, eg. stories. I wish I could inspire more people in the group to focus on personal writing. We often go off at tangents, talking about other things, even though these discussions are interesting. Are we more of a historical group than a writing group? Back home I relax and watch TV. Lots to think about.

27th April

I receive an email from Judith - it seems my book cover is causing problems. Bill cannot work with the file that Dave has sent him. Oh no! All I want is completion. This cover has already taken ages. I need to see the final result! It's a relaxing day. I watch a film in the afternoon. But in the evening I go cold and begin to shiver, even beneath my blanket. The shivering turns from cold to feeling intensely hot and sweating. By 10.00 I have hardly the strength to get upstairs, so I crawl up. I lie in bed sweating profusely. Then

I realise it's a fever - my temperature must have risen. I fall asleep.

28th April

I awake this morning feeling okay. The fever has gone, but my nightie is damp and smelly. I visit the toilet okay and prepare for a quiet, relaxing day. It's good. I eat well, work productively on my philosophy book, and enjoy my time alone. By bedtime I still have energy, and wonder about the contrast from yesterday. I feel so much stronger. From newborn kitten to lion? Could it be because this morning I held my bottle of holy water in my hands and prayed to our lady - leaning heavily on the strong, unyielding faith of the friend who gave it to me? Who knows? But I need all the help I can get.

29th April

I feel fine so far - fingers crossed for another positive day. We go and see, 'The Unlikely Pilgrimage of Harold Fry.' Tracey joins us - we haven't seen a film together for ages, so it's nice to have lunch and discuss the plot. The subject matter is a little close to home (terminal cancer) for both of us, but the theme of saving a dying person through faith is up-lifting and we enjoy the film.

I develop my draft of the philosophy book, on the conflict between freedom and the rule of law, and begin to wonder if, after three paragraphs about the effect of the French Revolution on law and freedom - whether this work is turning into a history book. Later, I watch TV and thank whoever may be out there for another good day.

30th April

It's my scan at 10.30. To my surprise I feel calm and relaxed as we walk through Christie's door a bit early. It's a strange process: drinking some special liquid for an hour, then bloods, then lying under this machine that tells you to 'breathe in and hold...then breathe normally'. After three repeats I'm done, then out after half an hour, to ensure no after-effects. My partner dashes off to his football match at Old Trafford, so I can write a little, read and watch 'Dr No' on TV. Wasn't Sean Connery handsome! All in all, a good day. The words of a poem float into my head - about hope, in the form of a butterfly that lands on needy shoulders to turn their darkness into light. I will work on it.

1st May

The Monday bank holiday. Family arrive early, 11.30, because my granddaughter, Paige, and her partner, Luke, who have been up north for the weekend, have to catch a 4.30 train back to London. We're caught unawares with the change in routine, but the day turns out to be delightful. I revel in the company of my whole family. We play Articulate, and the room is filled with joy and laughter. I feel well and completely at peace. By 7.00 they have all left and quietness descends. But it's okay. I smile and feel immense gratitude for what I have. Then it's TV, and bed.

2nd May

A day with nothing planned - so chance to catch up with my writing. I'm really getting into my philosophy book, enjoying exploring my deeper thoughts and beliefs, yet aware that I have so many projects on the go, I don't want to let earlier ones fade - my memoirs and reading booklet for the school still need editing for completion. As soon as my 'Lie' novel is out of my head, published and requiring only marketing, I'll get back to these two projects asap. I manage to send my review of Charlotte Levin's novel, and am looking forward to reading her second that Tracey has got for me. I manage four rows of knitting, watch the end of 'Malpractice' on TV, then bed.

3rd May

A lovely sunny day. It's our writers' meeting. I read the pieces that people have written, and begin my notes for the meeting. Then it's section 4 of my philosophy book - evil versus good. The writers' meeting is lively - with heated debate about philosophical issues. Then it's my usual - read, rest, bed. It's been an interesting day.

4th May

I awake with gusto, feeling good. I notice that my bowels have returned to their normal state, before I became ill - in both colour and consistency. Is this the result of eating better? It's ironic, just as I am beginning to feel okay again after my enforced rest, that my treatment may be due to restart in a few days.

No outing planned today. Plenty of time for writing. I feel fired up from yesterday's lively debate. Philosophy beckons! Maybe I can even pick up my paintbrush this afternoon?

About lunchtime I receive a phone call from a different hospital -

Manchester Royal. It seems they have already discussed the results of my scan (30.4) and wish to operate on my tumour. I am to consult with the surgeon next Tuesday at 12.00. I put the phone down and burst into tears. It's a shock, even though I have been aware of this possibility for weeks. Now that it is close, fear creeps in. My revised Will is not yet signed and sealed. What if...? But I must try to be positive. On the phone later, my daughters remind me that an op would not even be considered unless it was safe. They are right of course and I am being weak. Right now I need my strength. It will be okay! It will!

Later, my writing friend, Bill, drops off the second proof copy of my novel. I feel better, as I hold this work in my hand. I love the cover and can't wait to start marketing it. Imagine - my first work of fiction, after having written over twenty non-fiction books. It seems unreal. Will there be a sequel? Good question. If so, I will have to hurry up and write it. Time is not on my side.

5th May

I feel better today. I enjoy my Complan, Farley's rusk and banana for breakfast and settle down to my philosophy book. We go to Costa again for lunch - the highlight of my day.

I think about a new name for our writers' group - how about the 'Literary, historical and philosophical society', the LHPS? I am pleased to finish my poem on Peterloo, to read out at our next meeting. No painting and no knitting today! By early evening my energies have slumped again. But I'm well used to it now.

6th May

Coronation day. I am not a royalist, and my philosophy book will have a section on whether royalty should continue to feature in modern Britain. But today, I am curious and will watch the event in the background as I write and knit, and maybe paint? It is a strange day, almost like a fairy tale as I watch the pomp and ceremony, wondering what Europeans think about our over-indulged traditions. What does it all mean in this modern world? What has royalty got to do with religion? Does the Archbishop really believe that kings and queens are ordained by God? What will the King actually do to effect social and cultural change? I enjoy painting flowers in watercolour, having almost forgotten the joy of this creative art. The day passes in a strange way - neither a weekday nor a weekend. Just today - wedged between yesterday and tomorrow. Do I sense myself getting a bit morbid about my forthcoming operation? I must relax about it. Worrying will do me no good at all.

7th May
Sunday. I'm getting worried about my new Will, need it to be signed and sealed before my op. So I must ring on Tuesday to hurry the process along. Debbie and Tracey arrive about 12.30, for a chat and a knitting session. We play scrabble, before the grandchildren are dropped off by their dad. They leave early as Natasha has a birthday party to attend - trampolining. It's a pleasant day. I settle down in the evening to watch the coronation concert, and really enjoy it. Then bed as usual.

8th May
Monday bank holiday - I feel unsettled, not sure what my routine should be. It's not a normal Monday. We change the bedding and I do little tidying jobs, then settle into my writing again. There's nothing else on the agenda, but at least writing keeps my brain ticking over. It's a funny day. I write my charity cheques for the Mouth and Foot Painting Artists, people who have learned to paint using foot or mouth, because they have no hands. I have received their pack of birthday cards to purchase, and am in awe of the courage and perseverance of people who have overcome such life changing challenges. They give me hope.

9th May
It's hospital day - when my operation may be decided. We arrive early, but have to wait half an hour. I feel anxious sitting in the chair, until my name is called. The surgeon, a nurse and a dietician all ask me questions about my eating and emotional and physical strength. It is an uplifting meeting. I am reminded by the surgeon that it will be a big operation, which is why they want me to be as fit as possible before they do it. I leave the hospital with a number of leaflets about diet and exercise. Later I receive a phone call. Another hospital appointment, this time for me to have a fitness test (18th May) with the 'geriatric coach' - for over seventies. At the end of all this I feel much more hopeful and inspired. I am determined to improve my fitness, and start with a walk around the green. I have about two weeks to get stronger. I will be ready for that op!!!!

10th May
Wednesday - I manage 3 laps of the little green outside our house. Great!

Can I gradually build to 10? Even do a few skips with my rope? Writing as usual this morning. Must complete the reading booklet for the school, and send to the SENCO by Friday. It's our writers' meeting again. The weeks fly by. I have my philosophy piece to read out to the group for critique. Only five of us today, but it's a lively meeting. I do 10 squats and some stair-stepping, then a second walk around the green. Energy dips about 10.30, but I feel pleased with my efforts.

11th May

Thursday - very frustrating, not knowing whether the appointment at Christie's for today still applies, as we had a meeting on the 9th at Manchester Royal. However, I am feeling psychologically better, following Tuesday's meeting. Day begins with a walk around the full length of the green. Then I send my notes for the writing group. Today I will edit my reading booklet. I feel guilty that I have not been in touch with the SENCO to let her know how I am getting on.

I also read the stuff about diet and exercise that I was given on Tuesday. It's a shock - knowing that I will be under the anaesthetic for six hours, then will spend two weeks in hospital, and maybe have further chemo after that. I begin to understand how important it is to build my fitness before this event. I end up having a telephone conversation with the Christie's doctor, and I fill her in on what was said on Tuesday. She confirms that I am now under the care of Manchester Royal, and after the op will be transferred back to Christie. I manage a few squats and stair steps. It's a positive day.

12th May

Friday: I begin with a 20 minute walk. Fantastic! I ring about the Will, but am disappointed not to get through to anyone, again This delay is really bugging me. Writing as usual, then Costa again for lunch - with my second walk of the day from the car park and back. Just another day to get through. But I receive more letters from the hospital, for telephone appointments. I begin to feel overwhelmed, and confused with what is going on.

13th May

Saturday: yet another letter arrives, with an appointment at Manchester Royal with the 'Elderly Medicine' team. I almost laugh out loud- I have an appointment on 18th May with the 'geriatric coach', a telephone appointment on 22nd, with the surgery unit, another telephone appointment on 23rd with the dietician - then this visit on the 6th of June. My life is no longer my own.

Anyway, I must keep active, so try to get on with jobs: one cleaning task and planting summer flowers. It's a lovely warm day, and being in the garden is so relaxing. By the end of the day I feel better than I have for many weeks.

14th May

Sunday: I write a few notes about writing, as fresh thoughts always come into my head in the early hours when dozing in bed - so I feel the need to jot them down before they fade. Then I go into the garden to finish tidying my 'zen' area. I had forgotten how lovely it is to be amongst flowers - a source of mindfulness perhaps? Could part of this 'zen' area be my next painting project? Mmm?

In the afternoon, the family arrives. What bliss. Fun, frolics and knitting! Then it's TV again and bed - with a smile.

15th May

I awake with determination. First my walk. Then I enjoy and indulge in my writing projects, letting thoughts and opinions fly as freely as birds. We have a visitor today: Chris's nephew, Alex, who is passing through on his way to the Lakes. He and his mate are going to climb Hellvellyn. It makes me exhausted even thinking about it. I also tutor Nat for an hour, then enjoy my second walk back from his house. I feel tired but - Great!

I am getting angry about the delay with my Will. It's not good enough. My anger must have filtered through the airwaves - I receive a phone call to say it's ready to check, prior to signing. Hurrah! My stress and anger subside and I have a pleasant, relaxed evening.

16th May

I write as usual in the morning - editing my Reading training booklet. I have arranged to send it to Amanda to be published into a tiny booklet, perhaps to give out to libraries and other outlets, even bookshops. But before that I will send it to Kerry, the SENCO. I peruse my Will, then look at the questionnaire for an award I have been nominated for, to do with Education and Training. Odd! Who has nominated me - my publisher maybe? A mystery? I then compose a short note to my brother, Ian, to inform him of my cancer and forthcoming op. He will have been wondering why I haven't been to visit him. I feel better when I've posted it, but hope it doesn't cause him to worry.

Nothing else on the agenda today - it's read, knit, watch TV. But I am relaxed, as I feel my mind and body becoming stronger. I know that I will get through this.

17th May

Wednesday: Writing first (of course!). Then I read the pieces sent around by our writing group, and make notes on them. The session is interactive and satisfying, and I read out my poem on Peterloo, which inspires much discussion about the long struggle for democratic government.

After the writing group, I attend a Mindfulness session, at our local community centre, for an hour. This week's focus is the senses. First a few minutes of meditation. Then we touch, smell, taste, hear and see - describing each experience in turn as we go along. It feels good and I intend to go again next week.

18th May

Thursday - my appointment for the fitness checkup at Manchester Royal. But first, my writing. I develop my poem about 'hope'. We arrive in good time at 1.45 for the testing session, and I am put through my paces - breathing, finger grip, and the exercise bike. It's fun, and to my relief, the doctor pronounces me as fairly fit for my age group. He suggests some exercises - Nordic walking, stair climbing (at least five extra daily), and standing/sitting from a chair - how many can I do in one minute? It's looking good, and I expect to be fit for the op in about two weeks. He talks to me about it and I feel positive, reassured. I just want to get it over with, recover and put all this behind me.

After my session we go and collect my granddaughter from school. It feels good. We play checkers, have fun and enjoy our meal together. My daughter is not well - hay fever is affecting her eyes.

19th May

Okay - I start the day with Nordic walking. So far, so good. I'll do another session later this afternoon. Writing: I want to finish and send my reading booklet to the SENCO, and get my poem on 'hope' finished. It's a good, productive day. I do a second Nordic walking session, then some stair climbs. Great! I'm on a roll.

On the news tonight, we hear of the death of a pop star, at age 59, from pancreatic cancer. I sense a wobble coming on, and tears fall, before I remind myself that the death was a one-off. I will be okay.

20th May

Saturday: first my Nordic walking, then I go for my Covid jab. Then shopping, and home again. It's a beautiful, warm day, so I begin reorganising my 'zen' area in the back garden, and spend a lovely two hours manoeuvring pots and planting - ready to enjoy sitting out when the weather allows. It's hard work, pushing and pulling to move pots, but also good exercise, so I welcome it and feel a huge sense of achievement.

21st May

Sunday: Chris has gone to Birmingham to play his walking football, so I am alone most of the day. I start by Nordic walking, and can feel my lung strength improving. Then writing as usual. The girls come over for a while. We sit outside in the sun, chatting and knitting, before they both go off to a barbecue. I do some more planting and sorting in the back garden. My younger one returns later to collect the grandchildren, who are dropped off by their dad. The older one is stressed with her GCSE revision. I have forgotten what it's like to take exams, and what it feels like to be sixteen, with most of your years in front of you, rather than behind. We laugh and joke, and I am reminded that every small space of time counts. I must live in the moment and enjoy the time I have left.

22nd May

Monday - the gardener is coming to advise us on our mess of a front garden. My friend, Veronica texts to tell me to take omega 3, as it is known to slow down death from cancer - very uplifting! My list today, after this diary excerpt: send my Reading booklet to Kerry, write my Will notes and arrange signing, do a blog about the pros and cons of AI, and post mine and Judith's newly-published novels on Facebook. I must also write a review for Judith's, as she is writing mine. Wow - busy day. But then, I will be free to start editing my memoirs that are waiting in the wings. Another day of good eating, exercise and building up my strength.
PS. The gardener failed to turn up.

23rd May

Hospital day - at 2.00, then collecting our granddaughter from school. Full on. I do a blog about the sad state of education and unacceptable numbers of absentee pupils. The appointment is to talk with the 'elderly clinic' consultant about my operation. He asks me questions about health, exercise, eating and hobbies, and tests my memory. To my amazement, he also asks me about power of attorney (which I have arranged), warning me that after the op I may descend into a state of 'delirium', during which my attorneys may be needed - though I hope not! The meeting is positive and I come away feeling anxious to just get this op over with. It will be major. But I am told that my fitness is as good as it can be for my age group.

After school we take our granddaughter to the play park. She enjoys doing cartwheels on the grass, and we do 'stand/sit' exercises from a bench. Who does most in one minute? Grandad 40, Natasha 39 (determined not to be beaten) ! And me 22. I get the bronze. It's fun!

Tracey is a bit down today, about her own weight and fitness. The missing muscles in her core (replaced with "mesh') will always limit her level of fitness. I can only hope and pray that she can overcome this limitation, and accept it. Apart from this, she is healthy. Her cancer is at last gone. I pray that it never returns.

24th May

Wednesday. Our writing meeting. I phone the solicitor about signing the Will. Then get on with writing tasks and prep. I edit and send my blog, then post our two novels on Facebook, and edit/send Judith's review.

I receive a phone call from the hospital - a date for the operation - 23rd June at 07.15. So early? The date comes as a shock, a little later than I thought, but I then realise, giving me time to complete more tasks on my to-do list.

Our writing meeting is stimulating - we talk a lot about politics and humanities. I read out two poems which go down well, and inspire much discussion about poetry.

The Mindfulness session this evening is mainly meditation - very quiet and calming. I know that this will help me through this journey.

25th May

I start with my Nordic walking, and even jog a bit. Then settle down to my writing - my philosophy book. I receive a delightful email from Gemma, Head of English at the school I supported before this illness. She is thrilled with my Reading training booklet and wants to share it with colleagues at her forthcoming meeting with Literacy Coordinators, on behalf of Lancashire County Council. I am honoured and overjoyed that my work is so well received, and tell Gemma she can share it with anyone she likes, and do whatever she wants with the material.

We meet with the solicitor at 3.00 - a longer meeting than expected, while she goes through all the legal-speak for our Wills. Then, at last, the documents are signed, sealed and secured in the solicitors' safe (note my good use of alliteration). It's quite emotional, making a Will, especially in my current situation. Thank goodness, it's done and dusted. I relax with reading and TV for the rest of the evening.

26th May
Friday: I am on edge, wondering what time my appointment is on Tues, 30.5 - moved forward from 23.5, I think. I receive a letter for a pre-op assessment, Tues, 13.6.23. Is this instead of 30.5 - or as well as? I don't know. I have so many appointments, my head is in a whirl. There are no responses to our telephone calls, so I send a query by email and hope for the best. It's a quiet day - jog/walk, chair stands, another walk. Lots of writing! So, good overall.

27th May
Saturday: family coming over. I do some cleaning - bathroom, shower, porch, and feel good about that. It's a lovely, warm day, so we sit outside - talk, play cards, games and eat. Another lovely family day that I treasure.

28th May
Sunday - I wake up determined to make some headway on the house and garden before I go into hospital, because I know that I won't be able to do anything afterwards. I will be completely out of it for about six weeks from 23.6. How frustrating that is going to be - seeing what needs doing, but not being able to do it. I make a list of jobs for today and tomorrow - sorting out the summer house, getting rid of rubbish, planting in pots, feeding and watering. The weather is lovely so I must not waste it. No writing today.

29th May
Bank Holiday Monday - another beautiful day spent in the garden - about six solid hours of bending, pulling and shovelling fresh compost into the pots. I feel exhausted by the end of it - yet pleased with my efforts, and know that the doctors too will be pleased with me for building up strength. Tracey and the girls stop off briefly to show me the girls' new ear piercing. The almost-eleven year old says that it hurt and she cried. The piercing is her birthday treat.

30th May

It seems there is no hospital meeting arranged for this morning - it's me, getting confused again (confused.com must be my new name). So I settle down to some writing and try to feel calm and relaxed. Afterwards, we drop off some stuff at the charity shop, combining this with lunch at Costa. Later I realise that I could have gone to my art class, but forgot about it. An opportunity missed. Never mind, I must learn to get over things and not dwell on them.

31st May

Wednesday - how quickly these weekly writing meetings come around. I've got a new poem to read out, Non-communication. I have finished the 'politics' section of my philosophy book - I have so much to say, it has ended up quite long, so will prune it later, during the editing process. I go out into our summer house to do my writing. It's so quiet and peaceful - listening to the birds. A pigeon hops around the flower pots, as if to admire my work, then a squirrel saunters casually across the patio in front of me, before climbing the tree trunk, balancing its way across the top of the fence, and disappearing through tree branches. What athleticism! If only I had a fraction!

I drive myself to my meeting for the first time since my diagnosis. It feels good, and our meeting is lovely and interactive. Our writing group is becoming a friendship group, as we trust ourselves to talk openly. Back home, I sit outside with my book, enjoying the warm sunshine.

1st June

My time is approaching - twenty three days before the op. But I mustn't dwell. I have lots to achieve before the due date. A gardener comes this morning to look at our overgrown mess of a garden and offer advice on what to do. He gives us a price for having all the trees cut down by a third, and a huge 'bushy trim' at the front. I almost fall over at the cost but know it has to be done.

Lots of writing - I feel pleased. As well as my 'philosophy', I draft a poem about 'Life', to be read out at the next writers' session. I manage thirty 'chair stands' at one go - well done, me! The doctor from Christie's rings for our monthly chat, and I fill her in on my progress, and tell her my op date. She reminds me that I may need more chemo after. I shudder at the thought, then thrust it from my mind. What will be, will be.

Four rows of knitting, then I finish reading my novel, wondering how writers like Jodi Picoult manage to write such emotional stuff that grips readers up to the very last word. Reading is helping me to improve my writing.

2nd June
Another lovely day - reminding me to water my plant pots. A spot of rain would be so nice! I'm running out of Creon tablets, so ring the doctor to order more. It takes an age, but at last it's my turn as 'caller number one' on this odd system. Writing again, then I decide to add artwork to my poem on 'Difference'. It's ages since I've painted 'en plein air', in the garden - how mindful and relaxing. It feels wonderful. I water the pots once the sun has moved. Then I settle down to a new novel. So exciting! What would I do without my reading?

3rd June
I am alone most of the day - my partner has gone to play football (all the way to Grimsby). So, after my usual writing session, I do some cleaning, rubbish sorting, and get stones and pebbles for the garden. These last two weeks are a good opportunity to get jobs done before my operation. While it will be frustrating not being able to do anything at all, the more I can achieve now, the better I will feel.

4th June
Sunday - family visiting day. I jog a little through the woods this morning - the first time for many weeks. It feels good. I carry on sorting, cleaning and getting rid of rubbish, then arrange pebbles in the garden. To me, parts of the garden are like works of art - using shape and colour as creatively as painting a picture.

In the afternoon, Tracey and Debbie arrive. Another sunny day, so we sit outside and enjoy the warmth - knitting, much lively chat, then the girls get dropped off by their dad. Another family day to treasure - as my op looms ever nearer.

5th June
Coffee with my friends, Judith and Christine at 10.30. I walk around the green first, trying to move as fast as I can. Coffee with friends is lovely as usual, offering us all a chance to share our problems. I remind myself to socialise as much as I can before this op stops me from doing anything, and that I am not the only one with challenges. We all have significant

stories to tell.

6th June

MRI appointment, 9.40. We set off at 8.15, to allow for rush hour. The surgeon doesn't say much - just asks me a few questions, and I come away wondering why such a visit was necessary. Perhaps he just wants to look at me face to face, and judge how fit I am for the op. He tells me I have done well to get my weight back up.

When we get home, the gardener is working on our trees, cutting them down, chopping and tidying bushes. It looks neater, although we still have much tidying and sorting to do. It's not a good day emotionally. I hardly speak and am crying at frequent intervals throughout the day. I wonder if my depression has returned - as I sense myself retreating inside a dark shell from which I don't want to emerge. I see nothing joyful in front of me, but for the sake of my family, I know I have to pull myself together and climb this mountain. I have had two emotional breakdowns, the last in 2017. I must not - and cannot - allow another to take over my life.

7th June

It's our weekly writers' session again. How quickly they come around. There are only five of us, and I read out my piece about AI which inspires much discussion. It's my granddaughter's eleventh birthday - I ring at 5.15, to wish her Happy Birthday before they go to see the film 'The Little Mermaid'.

My Mindfulness session is illuminating - we are asked to write down stuff in life that 'drains' us on one side of a piece of paper, and on the opposite, stuff that 'sustains' us. I find this interesting. It makes me consider our domestic styles of living - how different they are, what limits (drains) my 'me-ness' and what helps me to let it out and even celebrate myself as a whole person. I explain this to the group, and find it helpful. This thought is worth exploring, as it lifts my low mood. Maybe I can learn to cope better with this situation.

8th June

Art this morning, for the first time in months - painting a picture of cows in a field. Love it. Danny, our tutor, has brought us all a bunch of sweet peas from his garden. They smell gorgeous. I decide to paint them later. Then I tidy the front garden - pulling up weeds and cutting down stray growth. We collect my granddaughter, Natasha, from school and she shows me her birthday gifts. One is a translucent, 'N' shaped key ring, inside which are yellow, dried flower petals. From September she will be walking home by herself from school, so will need her own key - again, a sign of growing up. The key ring is a beautiful, special thing. What a lucky girl she is.

My other granddaughter has enjoyed her last day at school, as she will attend 6th form college from September. Her school shirt is now adorned with colourful messages from her teachers and friends - as a lasting souvenir. She shows me her photos and tells me that it has been a sad, emotional day - the end of a chapter.

My daughter does my friend's novel review for me, because I couldn't. Thank goodness, it's now sent. A lovely, jolly evening that warms my heart.

9th June
Friday - I start with my Nordic walking and feel good. Then it's writing, as usual. I enjoy a delicious lunch at my friend, Jean's, house. I wanted to meet up before the op. We've lots to chat about. Then I manage half an hour of gardening.

My CT scan is at the weird time of 6.10pm. Trafford General is almost empty as we walk down the long corridor wondering where the X-ray section is. The nurse tries for ages to insert the tube that will send the 'dye' around my body, but my veins are so tiny, she struggles. I turn away, unable to watch as she inserts the needle, yet again. She says that the chemo will have reduced them. I feel more tired than usual when we arrive home, as I always do when we've visited a hospital. Trafford General is the fifth different one.

10th June
I awake determined to move forward with the house and garden. So I wipe around bedroom one - timing myself. Under ten minutes! Brilliant. Then it's the garden - remove dead plants, fill pots with fresh compost, plant and feed new roses. Maybe I will paint a little today - the sweet peas? I try, and enjoy the activity, but the artwork is not my best. I will try again. I am exhausted by all this activity. But feel good at the end of it.

11th June
Sunday: Party day to celebrate Natasha's eleventh birthday. The weather is great again, so we spend our time outside, playing 'Articulate'. Everyone brings buffet food - so no cooking. It's all delicious. How I treasure these family days. How many more can there be?

12th June

I look around the garden patch already done. I'm so pleased with it and look forward to working on the next patch today. It's all hard work but this physical activity is surely what the doctors want me to be doing - building up strength. First my writing, working on the garden, then I clean up the kitchen after yesterday's mess. I find myself praying for rain, just to avoid watering all the pots again.

Hallelujah! The ferocious storm that begins, thankfully just as I am putting my tools away, is anything but the gentle shower I expect. The heavy torrents weigh down the rose bushes, and the storm lasts for ages. But it's welcome, nevertheless.

13th June

Hospital day - again. We seem to be rarely away from hospital visits. It's my pre-op at 12.30. The nurse asks questions about my general health history. We talk about the op and she explains the procedure. She gives me a lung thing that I have to blow into four times daily to strengthen them. I have my bloods taken again and, to my amazement, it works on the second attempt. I book a Covid test for next Tuesday. Then that's it. Home, write a little and relax. Another day done, and I wonder how many more I have left.

14th June

Wednesday: our writers' meeting at 2.00. Another lovely, sunny day. It's gardening and writing again, as usual. We attend a brass band concert at our local church in the evening. It's nice to do something different. Most days everything feels the same, and I struggle to bring a sense of purpose into daily living. I try to lift the balls on my 'blower', but can't manage it, and haven't the patience to keep trying. I'll have another go at it tomorrow.

15th June

The fitter arrives with our new curtains but, to our dismay, they are still too short, so have to be remade - again. I go into the garden and finish off the patch, planting and laying cobbles. Then it's off to sleep at Tracey's to mind the grandchildren, as she is away overnight. I am struggling with the 'blower'. Maybe my technique is wrong? I'll ask Tracey how she did hers (following her lung operation last September). The sleepover is fine, we get ice creams, then fish and chips for dinner and enjoy a pleasant evening with the kids.

16th June

Friday - we set off home, after seeing the grandchildren off to school. It's Marcia's last day, just for her Physics exam, and I wonder what it feels like never having to enter the school building again - a new chapter for her. I feel depressed today but try to focus on my list of things to get done. 'Doing' is the only way to lighten my mood. It's writing first, then more gardening, on another patch. I have done a diagram, highlighting which areas I will be responsible for, and which my partner will deal with. The garden is huge, so we have to keep on top of it and I worry what will happen if I haven't the energy. I can't bear the thought of it getting overgrown, and all my hard work going to waste.

There is just one week now before the op, and the realisation is beginning to hit me. It's a major event, that will take me a few months to completely recover from, and I dread the chemo again. Will I ever get back to the fit and active woman I was? I wonder.

17th June

Saturday - we get up later than usual. I always feel adrift at weekends: not quite knowing how best to use the day. We used to visit the National Trust and enjoyed walking around the grounds before I became ill, but this year have cancelled our membership. We decide to go to Bent's and look around for a new garden bench, as the old one is broken (a bit like me). We have lunch, pick up more plants and compost, and do food shopping - then home. I spend another hour in the garden. The sky is grey. I hope for rain.

18th June

Sunday - I plant the new perennials and hope they thrive well in our garden: which needs their vibrant colour. Tracey comes over for our scrabble afternoon: a delightful, chatty session. We talk about my forthcoming op. She senses how nervous I am and tells me that after all her ops (five within nine years) she doesn't feel nervous any more. The girls are dropped off by their dad. It's the usual Sunday. Then the rain arrives and lasts for much of the day.

19th June

Monday: four sleeps until the big event. I find myself counting down, realising that I won't be able to do anything for a month at least after the op. It feels frustrating. I am a 'doer'. I like to get stuff done. This morning I manage some writing before going to the bank. I tutor Nat, for the last time for a while, and talk to Amanda about my reading booklet, that I've amended again. Sometimes I wonder why I'm bothering to publish it as a booklet. What will I gain from it?

My final tutoring session with Nat until September. I talk with Amanda about my R booklet and we agree to give it greater impact as a marketing tool, more booklet than leaflet - with a title page, and the front covers of my latest SENCO book and five parent books on the back. I feel better about it.

20th June

A busy day, with another hospital visit - this time for a Covid test. It's raining, so the garden gets another soaking. Then it's my art class - I'm pleased with my picture of a bee on a flower. Then we pick up Natasha from primary school for the last time, as she will be walking home alone from September, having joined secondary school. Another end of chapter for both of us.

To my surprise, Debbie joins us for a family meal at Tracey's - our last get together for a while. She cuts my hair short, as it's so thin and fluffy from the chemo treatment. Then it's home.

21st June

Is this officially the first day of summer? Planting again, then writing. My last session at the writing group. We talk about lots of things, but not much about writing itself. I read my 'Life' poem out, and it inspires much discussion. The Mindfulness session is about our primary and secondary responses to situations - reminding us of the need to be more aware of our primary responses, in order to handle negative situations better.

22nd June

My last art session for a while. I enjoy creating a portrait, using oil pastels. Then I work on the garden for the last time this summer, admiring what I have created, and hoping fervently that I will see my lovely flowers again. Perhaps I will paint each section of my garden while they are in bloom? Paige, my eldest granddaughter, phones to wish me well, and a lady from our art group pushes a get well card through my door. It's heartwarming to feel that people care. I phone Tracey, and she insists that Chris lets her know how I am as soon as possible. I can sense that she is worried - after all, she is my personal expert on cancer operations. My new Will, that has taken ages to sort out, is finally filed with the solicitor, helping me to feel at peace. Strangely, I feel calm, ready for this new interruption to my life and accept what the following months will bring.

PART 2: The Operation

<u>23rd June</u>
Friday - day of the op, when I half expect everything in my life to come to a halt. But I am ready. Let's get it over with. Afraid? Yes, very. I've been warned that this 'whipple' surgery is major. I know that half my pancreas will be removed, and its adjoining organs messed about with. I also know that I will be in surgery for about six hours. The information given to patients is so detailed these days. I understand why patients have to be given this information - yet, do we really need to know *all* of the sordid details, and possible side-effects?

Chris drives me to Manchester Royal, where I wait with other patients due to be operated on this day. I am allocated a booth in the admissions area, where the procedure is fully explained to us. As this is happening, Chris suddenly turns pale and leaves the room, unable to listen to all the gory details. I tell him to go home - that I will be fine. Then it's the pre-op stuff - and I know nothing more.

I awake, in the ward, encased in wires like the bionic woman: with a tube up my nose, drain in my side, and the catheter in. I can hardly move. But it's fine. Everything is fine! I have come through the operation okay.

<u>24th June - 5th July 2023</u>
I have to stay in hospital for twelve days. The bed is so uncomfortable, I can't wait to get out of it. It has a ridged (air rotating) mattress that is meant to prevent bed sores. I don't know whether to lie down or try to sit up - it's so uncomfortable either way. The nurses keep wanting me to sit in the upright chair by the side of my bed, but that's uncomfortable too. But what can I expect - from what has been done to my body? Rehabilitation will take time and there is no point in trying to run before I can walk. I will just have to be patient.

The food is awful. But I try to eat what I can. It occurs to me that there must be quite a lot of food wasted in hospitals. My bowels are completely blocked. I haven't 'been' since 22.6: two days before I came into hospital - at least ten days ago now. My stomach feels heavy and is distended. It's difficult to move with all the stuff hanging off me. The nurses keep wanting to get me sitting up in the chair, but that's uncomfortable as well. Stop complaining - I tell myself! Relax. Chill out. Let it all happen.

I am grateful for family visits, as well as Chris. Debbie and Andy visit me, then Tracey and the girls. A few days before I am due to leave hospital, they decide to move me into the 'eye' ward. I wonder why. They must need space in the main area. Unfortunately, this strange move occurs during visiting time - when Tracey and the girls are here. Natasha and Marcia find it funny, following the porters, as they wheel my bed through and around long, empty corridors, into a completely different part of the building, then into the small ward where I will spend my final three or four days.

The doctor tells me that I can leave hospital at last, and I am freed of all that paraphernalia attached to my body - apart from the drain, which the district nurse will take out later. I am ecstatic! So, I ring Chris for him to collect me. I can't wait to get home. But I have been well-cared for and again feel so grateful for our NHS, and for the skill of the surgeons who perform this kind of work. Imagine living in a country where this health system is not available. We must never take our NHS for granted!

6th July

Thursday: I'm home, but struggling to do anything. It's frustrating, not being able to do the washing, cooking or shopping. I even struggle to get upstairs - almost crawling up. Sleep is difficult at first, because I can't lie on my side. I can only lie on my back because of the soreness. But I know that each day will get a little better. The district nurse is going to come to give me injections every day for 30 days. At last! My bowels begin to move - but with a mind of their own. I dare not go far away from my loo.

7th July

I have 'been' four times this morning - urgently, but it's better than constipation. Halfway through eating a banana I suddenly throw up, and bring back everything I ate yesterday. It's so frightening, we ring 111 and get an appointment with the nurse at Salford Royal A and E. I'm checked out, spend the night in Salford, then have another CT scan. While I am there the nurse takes out the staples from my wound. We count them as she takes out each one - thirty one tiny metal clips, holding my flesh together. I am discharged around 4.00 pm.

Once home again, I feel wary about stretching the area where the wound is, in case it pulls apart. But, of course, it doesn't. It is healing nicely, and I marvel at the capacity for skin to knit together as quickly as it does.

The consultant at Salford has told me it will take months to get back to normal. So I must not be impatient - one day at a time. He prescribes

'Ensure compact' three times a day - small nutritional drinks intended to compensate for lack of normal eating. I arrive home determined to get back to normal - drink plenty of water, take more Creon tablets, eat better and try to do everything the medics advise.

8th July
Saturday: my day begins well. I feel positive - a bit of writing, walk around the green, watch a film on Netflix and read. Then it happens. Around 3.30, my need for the toilet is so strong I don't make it in time. What a mess! I'm cleaning myself up (as well as the loo) when I hear a knock- it's the nurse to give my injection. I open the front door not fully dressed, towel covering my lower parts and explain what has just happened. But I am not embarrassed - she is so lovely and understands the situation. But the incident frightens me and makes me afraid to leave the house. I end up wearing those Tena pants, intended for incontinence - just in case.

I begin to walk around our green for about ten minutes at a time. After a week or so, I can now lie on my side, and manage to sleep a little better. However, I am still not eating adult-sized meals, so 'thank goodness' for the 'Ensure' drinks. And it's so strange: all my life I have loved my British 'cup of tea'. But now, I can't drink it. Odd, isn't it? Foods that I have eaten and enjoyed for years are now (perhaps temporarily) off the menu - for example, eggs, cheese, tinned tuna. I don't understand it.

July and August
The rest of July is a write off, with August a little better. Everything stops. On some days I cannot even write my daily diary - or indeed write much of anything that makes sense. My head seems empty and foggy. When the weather allows, I sit outside for a while, read a bit, and just gaze at the flowers that I planted before the op. Their summer colours are so beautiful - representing every colour of the rainbow. I smile as I look at them.

The drain that has dangled from my side since the op, is taken off. At last my outer body looks normal, with nothing hanging from it. The nurse no longer needs to inject me. The area around the surgery is no longer sore, and I lie comfortably on my side to sleep.

Meanwhile I still have appointments with the dietician at MRI. He asks me questions about my eating - what I eat and how much. He says I am doing well, but reminds me to take more Creon with food. I realise how important it is to get back on track, ready for the next stage - eat more, drink more water, more Creon. It's up to me now!

I have my final appointment with the MRI surgeon, who reassures me that the cancer is out, and does not appear to have spread. This is marvellous news, but he also suggests that further chemo will help to ensure it does not return. I feel a sense of dread, knowing how affected I was by the previous chemo cycles. At the same time, I am reminded of my daughter's cancer experience - how her tumour returned more than once - and of her five operations, over a period of nine years. I know that I will have this second dose. The surgeon says that he is discharging me from MRI - returning me to the care of Christie's. He is pleased with my outcome so far, and I let him know what a great job he, and his team, have done.

Once again, I am more than thankful for our NHS. This year (2023) has been the summer of constant strikes by nurses and junior doctors for better pay. How lucky I have been to have my cancer so urgently, and efficiently, addressed since its diagnosis.

It's late August. My days are mostly the same. I try to write a bit, and am attending my writing group again after a few weeks of absence. I am walking around the green. Doing the 'sit/stand' exercises recommended by the physiotherapist at MRI. Eating slightly better - and the nutritional drinks are helping. I also manage a bit of cleaning or gardening each day.

Yet, on some days my mood is so low I struggle to do much - just lie on the sofa and hide between the covers of a novel. Books have long been my personal escape from reality - leading me outside of, and away from, my darker self - allowing me to retreat into fictional settings and immerse myself in the characters' problems.

I am still here! Living and breathing - and know that I am lucky.

PART 3: Post-op chemo

<u>22nd August, 2023.</u>
I have an appointment at Christie's to discuss my next cycle of chemo. I am weighed again, and have my bloods taken. The doctor, and nurses, are so lovely and I welcome their caring bedside manner. I am to have three cycles - each of three weeks on, one off - so 12 weeks in total. This treatment will likely begin early September and, if I sustain all three, will take me up to December 2023. Fingers crossed, that I can make it. A sobering thought. But again, how lucky I am, when I compare myself with people I see on the TV news - many thousands, millions even, many existing in war zones, with no quality of life - and little hope.

I receive a surprise - a huge shock, for which I am totally unprepared. Having asked the nurse how long I need to continue taking the Creon tablets, she informs me that they are to be taken for the rest of my life. I had not realised, having thought they were temporary until my system recovered. I consider this and now understand their essential function - as compensation for what has been cut out of my digestive system for ever. As I understand it, my pancreatic enzymes will no longer work on their own to digest food - hence the Creon. So I must remember to carry these where ever I go - anywhere that involves eating. It's okay - I will get used to it. I have to.

But for the sake of my emotional health, it is time to get back to being creative - as writing and painting are in my blood. They help me to move forward. I have lots of ideas, but can I see them through? Yes - I must!

<u>6.9.23 and 7.9.23</u>
Chris takes me to St Anne's for my bloods, and on the following day, the weekly drip. It's strange being back there. It was April when the doctor ceased my other cycle because of its terrible effect on me. The nurses remember my name from last time, so that's nice. I am weighed and the nurse reminds me to tell them if I feel unduly affected, as the dose is measured on the basis of height and weight. The drip itself takes the same length of time as before - about half an hour, but by the time the nurse has heated my arm ready, and managed to insert the cranula, and we begin - the entire process takes about an hour and a half.

The nurse reminds me that I will feel tired and gives me tablets for any nausea. He is right. All week I do feel more tired than usual. This is one out of the nine sessions - eight more to go.

13.9.23 and 14.9.23
I lie in bed thinking about time and how best to deal with its day-by-day passing, realising how, although we organise our daily lives around this constant measure, time is firmly in control. Our relationship is bound - yet, strangely separate. Odd perhaps to think that humans invented time as a more specific measure of night and day, yet time has now taken over to control us. As I stare at the digital clock on my bedside table, watching minutes change, I am amazed at how time now rules our lives. Something that we invented has a life of its own. A bit like AI?

But we can opt out for brief moments, according to the book I am reading on 'Becoming Supernatural'. According to its author, taking greater control over time, and being more in the present moment, has resulted in people becoming able to control their health - and diseases. So, can I improve my emotional and physical well-being simply by opting out of time's control - to be in the present moment? Can I simply 'be' in the here and now? This is difficult because my entire life has revolved around time: getting up, mealtimes, tasks to be done, appointments. For many of us, past and future have inhabited our minds far more than present moments - as memories, regrets, or negative feelings. But in order to deal, emotionally, with my cancer treatment, and to move into my final phase of life (old age) I need to place this in perspective with the external demands of time. I do not expect to regain what I have lost, in terms of strength and energy. I am lucky to be alive - but expect my future to be different than my past, health-wise at least, and must accept this change. While my cancer treatment has been ongoing, time has also been ongoing. When this chemo cycle ends - one full year of my life will have passed since I was first diagnosed. Is this the age-old cruelty of time: taking while never giving back? So, can I find some present moments that will help me to control time - and make my final years feel worthwhile and precious? Yes - that is my goal!

I am due for my bloods later today.

21.9.23
Thursday. An inner voice has been speaking to me - telling me to break free from everything to do with my past. Everything! Maybe it's the cancer voice - as a catalyst for change, firstly interrupting my life, emptying my head of all thoughts, stopping me from doing what I was; in order to guide me into

a fresh, new chapter. This means also breaking away from something that has kept me going and supported me through life's challenges for all of fifty years - education and teaching. But I am now heeding the voice. Yes, it is time for me to turn the corner and step onto a new pathway - become more free and unfettered - to write whatever comes into my head, in whatever form, for whoever will read it. And it's writing that will get me through this current interruption. For a while my head has been empty, completely void of ideas. But since that inner voice, I feel a stirring….almost like words are starting to build up again inside my brain. The words are a jumble. But they are there - waiting, ready to assemble themselves into some kind of creative form and structure.

How am I? My bowels have settled down a little - not quite as much wind. I feel more in control - less worried about making a smelly mess. Eating better? Yes, I think so. It's all up and down, but the little nutritional drinks (Ensure) are helping to up my calorie intake.

I have noticed a pattern with the new chemo cycle. I feel very tired for two or three days after, then a little less so for the next few days - up to the next drip session. So far, no other symptoms. So I can manage this. I know what to expect. This is week three - so six more to go. I can do it!

I'm having a PICC line put in at Christie's this afternoon, and am very nervous. In fact, I have noticed that every hospital visit causes a negative emotional reaction. I find myself trembling as I walk through the door to have something done. This line is to enable bloods to be taken more easily, as my veins have shrunk over the course of treatment. It will be okay, I tell myself.

22.9.23

Friday. The PICC line is fine - though my arm feels a bit tender. It seems strange to have this thing hanging out of my arm; for a few weeks, until late November, but I'll get used to it. It's at the top so it can't be reached without taking my jumper off - must remember to wear a tee shirt each time I go for treatment.

Today is not good - but starts off okay. My weight is 59.2 kg. That's not bad. But halfway through the chemo session my blood pressure plummets - I feel faint so they have to abort the treatment. After a few minutes they take my blood pressure and give me some fluids. Thankfully it's okay again. But it seems, I can't attend St Anne's any more for the chemo because they don't have a doctor on call. They explain that it's a safety issue and they can't take any chances. I understand, so the chemo will have to be at

Christie's. The nurse also explains that my bloods are a little down - 0.9. My immune system is a bit low. Oh well, that's how it is. Thankfully this is my free week, so I will try to recover a bit. Only six treatments to go!

8.10.23
Monday. We start again with the treatments. I have had a strange two days. Saturday was a day of nothing - with no energy to even get up from the sofa. Thank goodness for an interesting novel, followed by a daft episode of Midsomer Murders. I had a wobbly, having received further tablets to take, that are supposed to reduce the chance of me having another reaction to the chemo. I took one look inside the pack and burst into tears. Not more tablets! So now, it's thirteen at breakfast time, then more tablets and Ensure nutrient drinks later throughout the day. But, I read on the pack, these new tablets are only for three days. Good. Okay. Calm down. But is it three days before each dose, or three days before each cycle? Must ask when I go today.

Yesterday was much better - I felt stronger and more in control. It was also family day, and we had visitors from London too: Chris's nephew and niece, Alex and Sophie, on their way to a 'walking in the Lakes' holiday, so a lovely interactive day. But then came the shock! It wasn't until I went up to bed, and visited the loo that I realised my bowels had operated without me even knowing. I was horrified. Had it smelled throughout the evening meal, sat around the table with our visitors? Surely not! Clearly, I will have to wear the Tena pants for much longer, as my bowels still have independent minds of their own. I had felt nothing, so had no idea. On the positive side, I did feel stronger throughout the day. Was it those new tablets? Or is it psychological?

So, the start of my new three week cycle, today at 3.00. I try to think positive. After all, without all of this hassle, would I even be here?

10.10.23
Tuesday. To my amazement the new tablets have made me feel a lot better - stronger and less weak. I am less anxious about the whole thing. The chemo was okay - didn't feel a thing, and have no after effects. So, it's all fine.

16.10.23
Monday. It's been an odd week - up, then down. Once the steroid tablets wore off from Tuesday, my energy levels plummeted again from Wed. On

Friday, when I went for my bloods, the nurse took my 'obs' - the usual thing, blood pressure, temperature etc. They were all okay. So she has sent a message to Christie's to ask if my chemo dosage needs to be reduced a little in the light of my weakness. This morning I receive a call from the doctor. She asks me; do I want to defer the treatment for an extra week? NO! NO! I want it all over with as quickly as possible. She says nothing about the dose reduction. So, I will get on with this. I can cope with the weakness and tiredness for a few weeks.

18.10.23
Wed. It's the writers' meeting - and my first day without the steroid tablets. I feel weak but okay. Unfortunately, about twenty minutes into our meeting I start to feel strange. I can't focus properly and wonder if I am about to faint. Chris takes me home and to my horror, I discover that my bowels have worked again - without me realising. I clean myself up and lie on the sofa for the rest of the day. There seems no point in wondering how or why this happens. It just does - but thankfully only now and again. Three days to go before I can have my steroids again.

10.11.23
It is about a year since I first began to have my cancer symptoms, prior to the diagnosis. And so much has happened since. Today I have my appointment with the doctor at Christie's. I am anxious. A decision is to be taken - whether to continue with the chemo treatments or cease them. The nurse takes my bloods first, then we wait awhile. Another nurse then tests my blood pressure, temperature etc, as well as my breathing. All seems okay. Then I talk with the doctor about my symptoms - the weakness, lethargy and bowel issues. Then she says the words I desperately want to hear, 'I think we should cease the treatments.' Tears spring to my eyes and I try not to sob with intense relief. It is what I want, but I needed her to say it first, as her professional opinion. I needed her confirmation that missing those final three sessions would have little or no impact upon the likelihood of this cancer returning. As the surgeon had previously said, the tumour is removed and it has not spread. She confirms that I will have to take the Creon tablets, with my Omeprazole, for the rest of my life. But that is fine. I can adapt to that. I will also have a CT scan in a few weeks, and from then on, regular scans every few months or so. Before we go, the nurse removes the PICC line from my arm - and I feel free! Free!

The waiting room is strangely empty as we walk through the hospital towards the entrance for the last time. It's 6.15pm. It feels eerie, unusually still and silent. In the car as Chris drives us home, I think about what all of this means. But my mind is finding it hard to process. It's a shock. No more treatments! No more bloods! No more hospital visits! What will I do? How do I find myself again? I try to describe it but there is nothing around me but the vast expanse of an open desert. No signposts to direct me to where I want to go. I know where I wish to end up. I know the 'me' I wish to return myself to - but not how to get there.

But all around me is light. And light is hope! The sun is shining. Somewhere across that great emptiness of my emotional desert - lies my personal oasis.

And I WILL find it.

5.12.23

Weeks have passed since I became freed from the chemo treatments. And I am trying to move into my new post-cancer way of living. It's a slow process. My energy levels are still low and I spend much of my time lounging on the sofa: writing, reading, or watching TV in the afternoons. On some days, when the depression grips more tightly, I feel locked inside a dark tunnel with no door in sight. I struggle to see the new future, yet know that I cannot simply go backwards to pick up threads I left behind. They are broken.

The voluntary work in schools, that I was doing as the cancer hit, is sadly over. I will miss it, but now recognise that, after forty years, education can no longer be part of my life. Over the years, I have done what I can to influence and improve the life chances of children with Special Educational Needs and Disabilities through my teaching and books, and no longer have the energy to continue. Besides an octogenarian does not belong in schools. I must accept it and forge a new future. But I cannot yet visualise it. With the past obliterated, my head is empty.

I have almost completed my memoirs, and am trying to find old photos to accompany this work. As I sort through the piles of sepia-coloured images, life in a bygone age stares back, reminding me that I may not have many years left, so I must make the most of them. I am approaching seventy nine years old. The last chapter of my memoirs includes my imagined future: goals I will strive to achieve, in order to give my final years some purpose. Without goals, I cannot begin to take my first steps.

But first - Christmas! I will count my blessings at what this festive season brings for me: lots of family fun and togetherness. Then, 2024! Hopefully, a new start.

19.12.23

I attend the Christie for a CT scan. It is a strange feeling, walking back into the hospital and through its corridors after a few weeks of absence. I sense that negative energy again and remind myself that it is only a scan, and I know what to expect. Having registered my arrival, I am given the usual drink to take over the next hour. Then the preparation. Once in and under the machine, I close my eyes to ward off that feeling of claustrophobia. I hate small spaces - even lifts. Then that familiar feeling that I am about to wet myself, though I know I'm not - it's just the dye they inject me with. There is a warm feeling. I have to breathe in and hold, a few times. Then it's over and I just have to wait outside for fifteen minutes to ensure there are no after-effects. Then home. I feel exhausted but know that it is just an emotional reaction. Physically I feel fine.

I have a phone call appointment arranged for 5th January, for the results of this scan. It will surely be 'all clear'? Meanwhile there is Christmas to look forward to, and I will make the most of it, with our families.

I feel sad that my daughter is still not completely freed from her cancer journey. It has been over nine years since the original diagnosis, followed by chemo and operations. She has her scan on Christmas Eve - what a time! Then she is due for her results on the 19th January. So we are still in this together. I pray that both our results are clear and we can forget all about this horrible 'C' word.

6.1.24

How strange to be typing in the year 2024. It seems unreal: especially following this incredible year of 2023. The doctor rang yesterday with my scan results. Thankfully it's 'all clear'. I did not know what to say. There was a momentary silence on the line. 'Are you still there?' the doctor asked. 'Yes...yes,' I managed to blurt out. 'It's just ...difficult to take in.' I wanted to ask if they were sure about the result. That there had been no mistake. But I didn't.

Part of me had been expecting the 'all clear' - while the other part had been worrying that the entire chemo process would have to begin again. I know why this is. My daughter's cancer has kept on returning, and her seemingly endless, nine year, journey has taught me to expect negatives. I would not have been surprised if the doctor had said that my cancer had resurfaced somewhere else. But apparently it hasn't. I try to let this happy

93

news sink in.

So, I am now released from Christie's, into the after-care of Manchester Royal, for my six-monthly follow up scans, over a five year period. I smile as she tells me this. Will I even live for a further five years (from age 79)? I don't know how I feel. It's strange. Weird to be suddenly released from this captive experience. I imagine it as almost like being released from prison. Yet, I am free! I will be responsible for myself again. My partner will no longer be my carer. I will drive myself around. I will do household tasks. Yet, even the idea of all this seems odd, as I have hardly done anything for a whole year, since the chemo began, followed by the operation, then follow-up treatment. Cancer is not just physical. The chemo has affected my mind as well as my body. It has played a strange game with my emotions - tossing them into the air like balls being juggled. It has emptied my mind of creativity and writing inspiration. I have not painted. I have written very little. My imagination has been smothered.

But it's all good! Even my weight, at a size 10, is now good, and I must be careful not to put too much back on. I have *never* been as low as size 10, even when I first married at age 21. But it feels wonderful. Everything feels wonderful, largely because of my family and friends - whose support has been all around me.

So here I am, on the verge of my new life. I start writing in my new diary, which has a page for 'goals', and think about what I want to do, and where I want to go. My writing goals? How to get 'myself' on the right track to achieve happiness - who am I now? Am I any different to the person I was a year ago? Yes, in a way I am. I write down my personal goals. My writing goals. I think about what I want to change in my life, to reflect the new me. Am I stronger or weaker than the old me? Stronger, I think. More purposeful? Yes. Is this because I now realise how delicate health actually is, and how lucky I have been to have 78 healthy years before this journey began? Is it because life can be snatched away at any moment? So, I owe it to myself - the new me - to make every part of my life as good and positive as I can. For years, my emotions have been weaker than my physical body. It is time to even up the score. I am free - to be me.

19.1.24

I phone my daughter to ask about her scan results. Her situation is mainly positive, but pending something on her spine that is apparently unidentified. She is worried - her anxiety comes through as we talk. How I wish she could just have that wonderful 'all clear', as I have. She too deserves to be free -

after almost ten years of this journey (from April 2014). My daughter has recently had two scans: MRI and CT. Apart from the 'spine' mystery, everything else is okay - liver, kidneys, bowel - all shown to be clear of cancer. That's brilliant news for her, and for all our family, who have travelled with her. We now wait to see what the 'thing' on the spine is. Something to worry about, or just benign? The doctors say that it does not look like cancer.

20.3.24

It's been a few weeks. And I appear to be making progress. I am trying to build up my strength and do more tasks in the house. I begin to walk around the green outside our house: about 15 minutes each time, but it's a start.

Today I have a strange bowel problem. I rush to the loo at 5.20am, then have to go again at 8.20 am. My bowels have been getting a little better, and more normal, in recent weeks, but I now worry that something is going wrong again. No, I tell myself. It's just a one off.

Spring - summer 2024

I focus on gaining strength and placing the year 2023 firmly behind me. It is almost one year since the op. And I feel a little better. Life has not yet returned to 'normal' but I begin to wonder what my 'new normal' is - or ever will be. The new me? My energy levels and my bowel habits are still not back to where they were, and I am still not eating as much as I should. But am I expecting too much, I ask myself? Do I need to give myself more time to adjust? After all, both my body and mind have gone through a lot over the last year. I must be patient. My organs will take time to completely heal.

This summer my non-stop begonias, that I planted in the spring, are so beautiful. I stare at them constantly through the conservatory window. I plant them every year, but this summer their beauty has really shone through: with every colour of the rainbow. Are they a sign of the future, I wonder? I must continue to plant these lovely flowers each year. Their vibrant colours, even when struggling beneath grey, stormy skies - represent hope.

Autumn 2024

Here I am, almost at the end of my story. A new year and a new chapter to my life. As the summer of 2024 drifts into the autumn, I begin to feel more hopeful. On 11.11.24, I have a further scan. Thankfully, the result is again 'all clear'. Wonderful! I can now move into the future with confidence.

My mind is also clearing. I have begun to write again - and to paint. Our writing group has been focusing on the renowned artist, L.S.Lowry, who lived in Salford. Suddenly, I have an idea! An urge to copy one of his paintings. It takes me a few weeks, but I am thrilled with the result; an almost identical copy in watercolour of Lowry's work, 'Coming Home from the Mill.' One of my writing friends comments that it's, 'Er...more Lowry, than a Lowry. Superb.' I am inspired. At last I have painted something that I am proud of. The writing group suggest that it could form the cover for our next anthology, featuring all our 'Lowry' work. Brilliant - I will be so proud to see my artwork decorating the front of our anthology.

Well into November, a strange thing happens. I start to need the loo frequently; along with an uncomfortable, burning sensation each time I wee. I have to get up many times in the middle of the night: yet, each time, I release a mere 'spoonful' of urine. Odd! I wonder what it is and my mind starts to play tricks. Surely, it is not what I imagine? I go to the doctor, and a sample confirms that I have a urine infection. I am prescribed antibiotics. The infection goes away ...but the symptoms return after a few days. I am prescribed further antibiotics; this time, for two weeks instead of one. Again, the symptoms disappear. Then, to my horror, they reappear for a third time in just a few weeks. More antibiotics. Needless to say, my sleep is affected and I feel exhausted. After all this, the doctor requests an urgent ultrasound scan to check that there is nothing dreadful lurking 'down there'. As I lie on the couch, and the doctor feels around my tummy area and surveys the screen, I am assured that all seems well. We are now into December, and unfortunately, a further urine sample confirms yet another infection - the fourth. Yet, this time, I have no symptoms at all. Very odd indeed! At this point, I am still waiting to see what the outcome will be. Maybe my immune system is so low that I am now more susceptible to these kinds of infections. A friend suggests a daily drink of cranberry juice. So I try this. Every little helps, as they say.

December 7th, 2024
A month of activity! We have a happy event to lead me up to Christmas: my elder daughter's wedding on 7.12.24. Before the event, she asked me if I wanted to do some artwork for the tables: reflecting the '12 days of Christmas' song that we will all sing along to on the day. She loves Christmas (could she be descended from Santa?), and even her bridesmaid 'posies' are homemade, using colourful Christmas baubles. I happily agreed to the artwork and spent a month painting these images in acrylic:

to be glued onto silver backing along with the words to the song that Tracey has printed out, then slotted into stands and displayed. I feel proud of my work and Debbie is pleased too.

I have a posh outfit for the wedding; in a soft, dusky pink, silky, floaty fabric. And, get this - a proper wedding hat to match! I am fearful that this enormous hat will keep falling off, as it merely grips my head with an 'alice band' attachment. But it's fine, and throughout the day I feel more glamorous than I have felt for many years.

The day begins badly - with storm 'Garah'. I am taken by Chris to the Premier Inn, to join in the elaborate morning preparations. Debbie, Tracey, and younger granddaughters, Marcia and Natasha, are there, as is Paige, my eldest granddaughter, and Becky, who is Andy's (groom's) daughter: as the four bridesmaids. The floor is littered with makeup, clothing and all sorts of female stuff. I smile at the mess and clutter, and the amount of time it takes for the bridesmaids to make themselves presentable for this event. Hair curling! Makeup! What a performance! Marcia even does my make up. But, this event is so special, isn't it?

We arrive at Sale Registry Office for the ceremony. As I rush through the wind and rain, holding onto my dress with one hand, and my hat with the other, the photographer catches me in this strange pose. I enter and sit. The bridesmaids enter, then Debbie. The ceremony is simple, but lovely, and so different from a church service.

Yet, even this storm has not been able to spoil this beautiful event. Later, as I sit at the table, gazing at all the guests around the room, I feel love hovering in the air, like confetti, scattering a magic spell around the entire room: reminding me, and perhaps all of us, what weddings are all about. Love! The meal is wonderful too, and I manage to eat most of it. During the evening, I even manage to dance (minus the hat) when 'Let's Twist Again' is played. The bride looks her most beautiful, as do the bridesmaids, and I think how glad I am that Debbie now has a lovely and caring man to look after her for the rest of her life. I just know that they are right for each other. During the speeches, I am given a bouquet of flowers for my artistic efforts. A fantastic day that I, and our lovely family, will remember for the rest of our lives.

Christmas 2024
On Christmas Day most of our family gather at Tracey's house for a delicious meal and a thoroughly delightful day. Wonderful! Then, on Boxing Day, we all enjoy a second celebration at my house - with all of us

exchanging gifts that have been chosen with care and thought. Another day of love! My heart swells - I can hardly take it in. How lucky I am!

And all through December I have experienced none of the awful symptoms that I had been having earlier. Even my bowels are behaving better. Is this the turning point? Out with the old - in with the new. I hope so.

Epilogue: January 2025

January! A new year! What will it bring? As usual I am obsessed with goals; namely, my physical and emotional health, as well as writing, so I start walking again around our green. A good start to the year.

We begin with a sleepover visit; Chris's brother, Nigel and his wife, Helen, for 3 nights, from New Year's Eve. As always, I am anxious about the toilet issue with more people sharing them. But I have a plan B - the commode. It sits in the bedroom, almost daring me to actually use it. So far I have been lucky: as both toilets have been free when my bowel begins to self-activate. I try to enjoy the visit, and push my bodily anxieties to the back of my mind. To my relief, it turns out okay: we have a delightful three days of family catching up.

Of course, the year 2025 really kicks off to a good start with my birthday - 80 on 2.1.25. Imagine! I wish I could stop the clock, as eighty seems a horrible number to reach. Chris has booked a meal at Albert's, and most of our family attend. What a surprise! There is even an '80' balloon fluttering on the table, to greet me as we walk into the restaurant. After the meal, I even have a cake with candles. It's all so touching, as I realise what they (mainly Chris and Tracey) have done to make me feel special. This event is so enjoyable: huge waves of love flow over me. I take the balloon and the cake home. And open my gifts there. How lucky I am. Amongst my gifts, my daughter and younger granddaughters (Marcia and Natasha) present me with a surprise: an album with the story of my life in photos, starting with me on my mother's knee as a baby - all the way through, to now - even with a wedding photo from Deb's 7.12 event. Eighty years of me! I smile, then realise how clever they have been. A few weeks ago, I was asked if they could borrow my box of old photos for the children to look through: never imagining the real reason why they wanted them. Now, as I write about this on the 16th, the balloon, while less plumped up, and losing its helium - is still standing. Just about. A bit like me really.

Again I remind myself how lucky I am. On 4.1.25 I watched a programme on Channel 4: 2024 from the air. It was an outline of the whole year, featuring the wars in Gaza and Ukraine, multiple climate change events, as well as the political landscape. It made me feel sad, realising what is happening in our world; the battles between humans and nature - as well as between humans and other humans. Why? There are no answers. So why do I keep asking this same question? As the world turns, no-one with the power to put things right appears to be gazing towards the distant horizon: politics is still about greed and growth - the here and now, as if our planet can take care of its futuristic self without any human help. If only it could!

Back to me and my family - with much to smile about. Marcia is doing so well at college, and intending to study law at university. Natasha is doing well at school, now in Year 8, and in the top set for most subjects. They are both working hard, and seem to have grasped the message we continually pump into them: that education is a key to the future - opening doors to life chances, choices and opportunities.

Chris is happy with his walking football - it keeps him fit. Hopefully, we can pick up with our social life again; with the occasional film and theatre play? But can we go on holiday again abroad, as the insurance for me may be sky-high? We will see.

My brother, Ian, is recovering from his bladder cancer, having had radiotherapy, but no operation so far. Another 'all clear'.

And Tracey? She has met with the surgeon who inserted the 'mesh' in her tummy area. He could not find anything to account for the pain and discomfort that she is still experiencing, and has recommended 'pain management' therapy. So she is going along with that. After all, the fact that she has been examined and he has found nothing amiss, is surely positive. All is mainly well and, like me, her goal is to improve her fitness levels. We must help each other along.

My writing? Thank goodness, the cancer didn't interrupt completion of the SENCO book (published by Routledge, Dec. 2022), but I must market this work more. My self published books sit on the shelf, also awaiting media attention. This is one of my main goals for 2025 - to market my books through social media: my non-fiction book, 'Time of the Virus' (2021), my first novel, 'A Lie Never Dies' (2023), Memoirs (Spring 2024) and finally, 'Becoming a Reader' (Dec 2024). This latest non-fiction work has been a labour of love: expanded from the work I was doing in the secondary school, and aimed at encouraging and supporting teachers, teaching assistants and other adults, including parents, who seek to improve reading standards. The delightful cover picture has been produced by Chris's brother, Nigel.

But in order to sell any of these books that currently float (unnoticed) in that enormous Amazon ocean, I must adopt some media discipline. My website, posts and blogging have all been sorely neglected of late. So, although I do not enjoy this aspect of authorship (I would rather just compose), my message to myself is - marketing. Marketing! Marketing!

And the more pleasurable side of writing? My sequel to the 'Lie' novel is almost finished: as is this 'C' diary - both hopefully for publication later this year. 'Becoming a Writer,' the 'sister' book to 'Reader' is developing for next year. Waiting in my writing wings, partly done, are my books on Poetry and Philosophy. So I have plenty of writing to fill my time happily for another two or three years at least.

But the highlight of 2025 has to be my granddaughter's wedding in Italy (October) - a four day event, with a few more days travelling around Italy. Just thinking about it makes me feel quite exhausted. Yet, I am thrilled at the prospect of our family being together again in such an exotic place. It will be wonderful! My first holiday abroad since June 2022 (before this cancer interrupted everything).

So, I must get fitter for this key event, mustn't I? Walking, sit/stand exercises, stairs and yoga - all these activities must begin to feature in my daily life. The wedding will surely inspire me to make the effort. October - here I come!

On 28.1.25 I attend the doctor's surgery for my 'bloods' to be taken. The nurse manages to extract the sample on her first attempt. Hurrah! That means my veins have returned to their normal size again. My blood pressure is okay too. And I have put on weight - to 9 stone, 2 lbs. Brilliant! I relax in the knowledge that all seems well.

The Chinese zodiac on Jan 29th announces the year of the wood snake; marking a period of wisdom, adaptability and transformation. The snake is known for its intelligence, strategy and charm: while the wood element brings flexibility and creativity. I just love it! Maybe I can assimilate all of these 'snake-like' attributes into my own human persona, and carry them forward towards my personal transformation? Why not? It's all in the mind.

Meanwhile, that little bottle of holy water given to me by a friend? It still sits on my bedside drawers, where I see it daily - a heart warming symbol of spiritual faith, even though it is beyond my understanding.

We all have challenges of one kind or another. That's life! And I feel so lucky to have triumphed over my personal challenges, albeit with the help and support of my dear family and friends. Thank you all!

Finally, when my time comes, may I die with a pen in my hand (or my fingers over the keyboard)?

Here's to a happy and healthy future for all of us!

Sylvia Edwards has also written

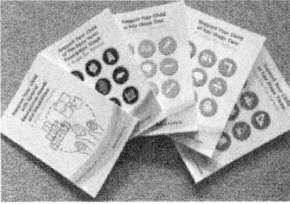

Parents: Help Your Child Succeed
A series of five books aimed at inspiring parents to become more involved in education:
SEND
Early Years Foundation Stage
Key Stages 1, 2 and 3.

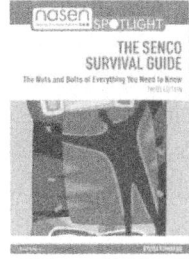

The SENCO Survival Guide
ISBN **978-1032219479**
SEND policy for schools:nuts and bolts of everything you need to know

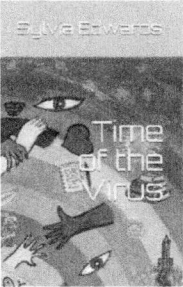

Time of the Virus.ISBN: 9798541841855
Is what IS how it must always be? Let's make our world a better place. Complemented by poems, stories and artwork, this book debates key issues, eg. racism, religion, politics.

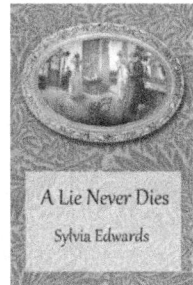

A Lie Never Dies.   ISBN: 979-8387509599
1901. This novel charts the dramatic consequences of a lie that drags Kristina through a maze of emotional challenges, changing her life forever. Can she find lasting happiness ina world where she does not belong?

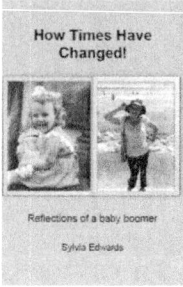

How Times Have Changed! ISBN: 9798877331617
These memoirs attempt to bridge the post-WW2 world with today's technological version. Yet, in 2024, as wars still rage, I wonder if humanity is any different than it was - or ever will be. Against this backdrop, I have told my personal story with honesty and sincerity and hope that my version of truth reflects what was.

Becoming a Reader ISBN: 9798302216953
Schools need to do better. Research continually informs us that far too many children are not reading as effectively and efficiently as they should on leaving primary school; thus limiting their secondary cross-curricular achievement. This book encourages all of us; government, schools, society and parents - to work together and ignite that reading flame for all young people! Every child a reader!

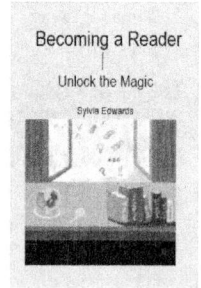

Sylvia Edwards has also contributed stories, poems and memories to the many publications of the SWit'CH creative writing group

I

My Life and Other Misadventures   ISBN 978-1-326-60665-7
Alan Rick
A collection of humorous and poignant nostalgic reminiscences covering Alan's early school years in the war to national service in Egypt. Alan looks askance at the society of the day with a wry, knowing, smile.

Switch On, Write On, Read On   ISBN 978-1-326-73048-2
Approx. 200 page the first showcase of the group's creativity. Containing nearly sixty humorous, whimsical, thought-provoking, ironic, and eclectic writing.

A Write Good Read   ISBN 978-0-244-73623-1
Tales from Swinton and Salford; the Wigan train and around the world drawing on the experiences and interests of the group. Modern telecoms and IT feature, so do the Ten Commandments and seven dwarfs. Historical pieces range from the industrial revolution to individual childhood memories.

Peterloo People   ISBN 978-0-244-18472-8
A potpourri of passions gives the reader the chance to walk in those shoes to the peaceful protest, the actions on the day and shameful reaction afterwards. But the focus is not only on the victims; the perspectives of the authorities and militia are treated with sympathy and criticism in due turn – and there's even a wry tale of hope and salvation for a government spy.

The Taste of Teardrops   ISBN 978-0-244-26569-4
A Novel by Judith Barrie.
A gripping psychological thriller set in a sleepy seaside town. It's 1981 and a young woman settles into her cosy new home believing that she had found peace and tranquillity after a painful marriage break-up. But there are mysteries. Who is the woman upstairs and the irresistibly attractive man who visits her?

Memories Unlocked   ISBN 9798570919617
These childhood reminiscences of localities now gone, holidays, school, nature notes, plane crashes, sex education and walking home after dancing form part of the mischief, mayhem and misadventures of our young lives. Drawn from the experiences of SWit'CH writers in their formative years.

Selected Memories   ISBN 9798598323212
This choice of writers' recollections taken from Memories Unlocked follows
on from The Big Switch, which was produced for those with a visual
impairment, with a font developed by RNIB. The book is easy to handle. Big
letters on low contrast paper make it an easy read and a 'page turner' in the
literal sense.

War and Peace in Pludde Bailey   ISBN 979-8391352990
A Novel by Judith Barrie
Pludde Bailey an old fashioned village. There was a public house where
men gathered to argue; a corbner shop where the women gathered to
gossip; a quaint little chiurch up on the hill. Occupied with blackout curtains,
rationing and air raid shelters, not one of the inhabitants suspected that they
harboured a fledgling killer or that he would kill again nearly twenty years
later.

The Big Switch   ISBN : 9798644090433
A collection of short stories in large print format for readers with a visual
impairment such as Macular Degeneration or Glaucoma.
'The Big Switch' is a compilation of extracts from some of the group's
previously published works. Designed for easy reading.

A Pain in the Bum   ISBN: 9798590032099
Veronica Scotton
The author's words say it all "I was so very fortunate, not to have to face my
cancer alone. Whenever I began to feel overwhelmed, the rock who is my
husband was by my side. My children and grandchildren lifted my spirits by
being positive about the whole thing and my siblings and friends with their
humour, often black humour gave me the best medicine."

All Kinds of Everything   ISBN 9798371732019
A collection from the 2023 team of writers. Stories and poetry
complemented by members reminiscences. As new members join us, our
versatility and variations expand. This collection compares well with the
standards established and maintained over the years of the group's
successes.

Printed in Great Britain
by Amazon

61853003R00060